P9-DHQ-555

THE BOOK OF

Potpourri

Fragrant flower mixes for scenting
& decorating the home

THE BOOK OF
Potpourri

Fragrant flower mixes for scenting
& decorating the home

PENNY BLACK

Photography by Geoff Dann

SIMON AND SCHUSTER
New York London Toronto Sydney Tokyo

To Bob

Important notice
*This book contains recipes using dried flowers, herbs, and other
ingredients that, when mixed properly, are perfectly safe.
However, certain of the contents may cause an allergic reaction in
some individuals, so reasonable care in the preparations is advised.*

Simon and Schuster
Simon & Schuster Building
Rockefeller Center
1230 Avenue of the Americas
New York, New York 10020

Senior editor Jane Laing   **Art editor** Gill Della Casa
Editor Sean Moore   **Designer** Caroline Mulvin
Editorial director Jackie Douglas   **Managing art editor** Alex Arthur
Photography by Geoff Dann   **Art director** Roger Bristow

Simultaneously published in Great Britain by
Dorling Kindersley Publishers Limited,
9 Henrietta Street, London WC2E 8PS

Printed in Italy by A. Mondadori Editore, Verona

3   5   7   9   10   8   6   4

Library of Congress Cataloging in Publication Data

Black, Penny.
   The book of potpourri.

   Includes index.
   1. Potpourris (Scented floral mixtures) 2. Aromatic
plants. I. Title.
TT899.4.B57   1989   745.92   89-4312
   ISBN 0–671–68210–5

Contents

Introduction

Throughout my childhood, which was spent in the English countryside, I enjoyed, and was fascinated by, the scents of the wildflowers and, of course, those of the fragrant old roses, flowers, and herbs that grew around our little thatched cottage. I never passed southernwood without tweaking a leaf, nor could I resist lemon balm and mint. Floppy old roses were crammed into jars and placed beside my bed. All my childhood memories are embalmed with the gentle perfumes of our garden and those of the surrounding road-sides, meadows, and woods. However, nobody mentioned potpourri to me and I did not really become aware of such a thing until I visited the American Museum at Claverton Manor, near Bath. The beautiful bowls of potpourri on display there opened a whole new world to me, and I left with an obsessive interest in the subject that was to change the course of my life.

The ancient art of perfumery

Perfume has probably always held a fascination for humanity. The burning of scented woods gave pleasure to our earliest ancestors, and, in fact, the word *perfume* is derived from *per fumin*, meaning "by means of smoke." The earliest records of the art of perfumery are those of the Egyptians: sweetly smelling oils prepared from flowers, herbs, and spices played an important role in their daily lives. The oils were used to appease the gods, scent the air, anoint the body, and even embalm the dead. The perfumed resins, frankincense and myrrh, along with other aromatics, were burnt as offerings to the gods, and some of the beautiful alabaster vases that were found in the tomb of Tutankhamun, more than 3,000 years after they were buried with the young pharoah, contained unguents that were still fragrant.

Decorated scales
This pretty piquant herb potpourri, decorated with anemones, ivy flowers, and yellow potentillas, makes a stunning visual feast when displayed in a dish from an antique pair of scales and hung at the kitchen window.

The Greeks and then the Romans learned the sybaritic pleasures of perfume from the Egyptians. Interestingly, most Greek perfumiers were women, although it was a male naturalist by the name of Theophrastus of Eresus (fourth century B.C.) who first wrote of the ingredients used in perfumery. Many of them can be used in the potpourris that we make today: roses, clove pink (whose flower perfume includes the scent of cloves), bergamot, thyme, myrtle, marjoram, orris root, cinnamon, and cardamom, to mention but a few. When the Roman writer Pliny spoke of perfumes, he mentioned coloring them with the red dye of alkanet, one of my favorite flowers, whose little blue blossoms peer at me from the nooks and crannies of my cottage garden.

The growing use of aromatic plant material

With the fall of the Roman Empire, perfume continued to be used in the West only for religious celebrations by the Christian church. The Arabs, however, continued their scientific research into aromatic plant materials and perfected the art of distillation – the separation of the essential oils from the fragrant elements (see p. 122). This achievement revolutionized perfumery, for the concentrated perfume of an essential oil plays the most important role in the creation of the bouquet of a mixed scent. The most important essential oil is that distilled from the petals of the highly fragrant damask rose, and which is known as "attar of roses." Today we can all grow damask roses and use the petals in our own potpourris.

Throughout the Dark Ages, aromatic plants and herbs were grown only in monastery gardens, and these were, in fact, the only means of medication available at that time. However, by the sixteenth century, an enormous range of scented materials was available to the housewife, brought into Europe from the Levant by the Crusaders. Many large houses of the period had a "still-room" – a small room set apart from the kitchen in which a stove was always kept burning. In this warm atmosphere, the housewife dried and stored the fragrant plant material from her garden, together with the imported aromatics.

It was in the still-room that the mistress of the household, or perhaps a maid, made all the preparations that kept the family healthy and clean, and the house and clothes smelling sweet. She strewed some of the dried herbs, such as elecampane, sweet flag, and bay, on the damp, musty floors; she made washballs and polishes; she ground fragrant powders and put them into small bags to place among the linen; she concocted cordials, tinctures, and ointments from recipes passed down from mother to daughter; in fact, the health of the family was

The rose bowl
This lovely china washbowl is filled to overflowing with opulent pink and red roses, lavender, mixed herbs, and cinnamon sticks. Totally traditional in concept, this rich, rosy potpourri, known, in years gone by, simply as "the rose bowl," will perfume even a large room.

dependent on the ability of the housewife to dispense these herbal remedies. A few of the early recipes can still be found in Mary Doggett's seventeenth-century book, published in the UK and entitled *Her Book of Recipes*.

The development of potpourri

Although homes were already being perfumed by mixes of scented flowers, herbs, and spices by the sixteenth century, it was not until the mid-eighteenth century that the term *potpourri* came into common usage. Originally "potpourri" was a culinary term meaning a stock-pot of mixed vegetables and meat (its direct translation is "rotten pot"), but during the eighteenth century the phrase came to mean a mixture of scented plant materials that were used to perfume the home. Rose petals were the most important ingredient, hence the term *rose bowl*, and were almost always used in the early recipes. However, scented orange flowers were often mixed with rose petals, and no doubt the housewife experimented with any dried flowers that retained their fragrance. Spices and fixatives were also included, the latter often being of animal derivation, such as musk, civet, ambergris, and castor.

The traditional potpourri contained the following five groups of ingredients: scented flowers and petals, or woods, roots, and barks; herbs; spices; fixatives; and essential oils. Today, potpourri has the same constituents, although we tend to use vegetable rather than animal fixatives. There is really no mystique surrounding the making of potpourri and the proportions of ingredients in every recipe can be varied enormously, depending upon what is on hand. However, it is true to say that you will always require most material from the first group, which will set the

China shell
This Victorian china shell is filled with Rosa 'Tour de Malakoff', Rosa alba 'Celestial', *and exquisite little mixed rose buds. Pretty green roundels of ivy flowers and mixed green herbs complete the pretty, old-fashioned mix, and floral essential oils add to the light, sweet perfume.*

theme of the mix. These days we include many unperfumed flowers to improve the appearance of a mix; in the same way we also incorporate brightly colored, or intriguingly shaped, berries, slices of dried exotic fruits, and seed heads. We rely much more than our ancestors on essential oils to impart the fragrance of our choice to each mixture.

There is a tendency nowadays to introduce nonfloral scents into our homes, such as fruity and oriental perfumes, or the more mellow notes of balsam and wood, but the fragrance of a potpourri depends entirely upon personal taste. A potpourri today can be richly traditional, flowery, woodsy, musky, fruity, or it can even emit a deep, masculine perfume. Visually it can consist of shades of one color, look highly decorative, or be just a lovely chintzy mixture. I never tire of mixing and sniffing! To me there is no lovelier artistic medium than flowers, and I use the delicate dried blooms and leaves to create wonderful collages of color, texture, and shape. The perfume of the garden can be immortalized in the faded, papery beauty of the dried flowers and leaves of a potpourri. The petals may have lost their moist bloom and heady fresh fragrance, but there remains an exquisite charm and shadowy perfume in the delicate dried blossoms.

The versatility of potpourri

Potpourri can be displayed in many different ways: china bowls and dishes, glass containers, antique wooden bowls, large shells, baskets, lidded jars, and boxes – the list is endless. It can also be used to perfume sachets, cushions, nightdress and handkerchief cases; soaps can be stored among potpourri, where they will absorb

Country basket
Decorated with sprigs of white anaphalis flowers, this rustic basket is filled with pine cones, conifer tips, sandalwood shavings, citrus fruit, lavender, and various spices.

Porcelain dish
An exotic potpourri with a rich, fruity, oriental fragrance, this mix is composed of delicate dried slices of kiwi fruit, strawberries, and star fruit, combined with citrus peel, lavender, and yellow and purple flowers.

the fragrance of the mix; writing paper, cards, and drawer liners can be packed between layers of potpourri and they too will become perfumed. Bath sachets can be made from both herby and floral mixes, and tussie mussies, baskets, and garlands can be scented with little net balls of potpourri. Sleep pillows can be stuffed with soothing hops and lavender mixes. Sachets can be suspended in cupboards or on coat hangers, packed in drawers, hung from door knobs, or propped on shelves. Tangy and decorative pomanders can fill baskets or be suspended. In fact, there is nowhere in the house that cannot benefit from the delightful natural perfume of these aromatics.

The methods of blending fragrant materials

There are two methods of making potpourri: the dry method and the moist method. The dry method is by far the quickest, easiest, and most commonly used. The dry plant material is mixed and used as soon as the ingredients are ready and available. Most of the potpourris shown in this book are made by the dry method, for there are infinitely more recipes that can be concocted using it. The moist method requires more patience, as partially dried fragrant petals and flowers must be cured with natural salt (and sometimes brown sugar and brandy, too) before mixing them with the dried herbs, spices, fixatives, and essential oils. Visually, a moist potpourri is not as attractive as a dry potpourri, but the fragrance is hauntingly rich. Traditionally, it is displayed not in open bowls, but in lidded potpourri containers that can be opened whenever the delicious fragrance is required to perfume a room. Alternatively, you can bury a muslin bag of moist potpourri in an open container of dried flowers, or display an open bowl of a moist mix covered in decorative dried blooms.

I have adapted the recipes suggested in this book from traditional mixes and from potpourris that I have made myself. I tend to favor rather rich perfumes, and frequently use small amounts of frankincense, myrrh, and patchouli oil, as well as other more lightly scented essential oils. More recently I have experimented with woods, roots, and seeds, with some stunning results.

A feast for the eye
Sitting on the table is a silver dish of roses, plates of yellow herbs, a box of exquisite, pale blossoms, a pretty wedding potpourri, and a sumptuous dish of flamboyant peacock potpourri.

CHAPTER ONE

Scent on Show

*T*his chapter contains forty recipes of many different
scents and appearances. There are chintzy mixes
with floral fragrances; pretty herby potpourris, smelling of
lemon or mint; hauntingly rich moist mixes; traditional
damask rose bowls of rich blooms; and many other
tantalizing recipes. In each recipe you will find five main
groups of ingredients: the fragrant flowers and petals, the
herbs, the spices, the fixatives, and the essential oils. Every
potpourri contains material from each of these groups. The
quantities I have given will fill a medium-sized mixing bowl
and refer to *dry* measures. Potpourri can be made using one
of two methods: the dry method (see p. 96) and the moist
method (see p. 98). I have included many more recipes that
call for the dry method, as it is far easier to make potpourri
by this means, and the results are much more attractive
visually. However, a good moist mix has an unsurpassed
fragrance, and I have included a few recipes under
"Heady Aromas."

The rose bowl

The beautiful petals of dried roses formed the basis of the very first potpourris to be displayed decoratively in open dishes or bowls.

The beauty and perfume of the fresh rose and the elusive sweet fragrance of its dried blooms and petals captivated women and men from the start: no flower has been used so consistently for both adornment and perfume. In fact, the faded-parchment beauty and lingering sweet smell of the dried rose are largely responsible for the origination and development of potpourri.

Although the spices, oils, and fixatives included in a "rose-bowl" potpourri alter the nature of its perfume, the underlying scent is always that of a dried and perfumed rose. The old-fashioned damask and centifolia roses have the strongest perfumes, but any rose can be dried and used in a potpourri; the addition of a few drops of rose oil will more than compensate for any lack of scent in the blooms. Introduce other scented and dried flowers to a rose-bowl potpourri to provide color variation and to alter the perfume subtly. Of the four rose-bowl recipes shown, the rose and garden-flower potpourri has the lightest perfume, although it still contains the evocative sweet bouquet of an old "still-room" recipe, and the rose and scented-leaf geranium potpourri has the sharpest, the geranium leaves and the rosemary adding piquance to the soft fragrance of the roses. The rich rose potpourri is the most traditional of the four.

❧ RICH ROSE POTPOURRI ❧

1 quart rose petals and blooms
2oz lemon verbena
1oz lavender
2 teaspoons cinnamon powder
1oz orris root powder
½ teaspoon whole cloves
¼ vanilla bean
5 drops rose oil
2 drops lavender oil
1 drop patchouli oil
rose blooms and rose leaves to decorate

A traditional, time-honored "rose-bowl" mixture with a rich and evocative, sweet, rosy perfume.

Lavender

Lemon verbena

Lavender oil

Rose oil

Patchouli oil

Cinnamon

Orris root

Rose blooms and rose leaves to decorate

Cloves

Rose petals

Vanilla bean

ROSE AND
SCENTED-LEAF GERANIUM POTPOURRI

1 quart rose petals and blooms
2oz scented geranium (pelargonium) leaves
1oz rosemary
1oz orris root powder
½ teaspoon whole cloves
½ teaspoon ground allspice
½ teaspoon grated nutmeg
3 drops rose oil
1 drop rosemary oil
1 drop geranium oil
rose blooms to decorate

*A slightly spicy, traditional rose recipe decorated with rose blooms.
The perfumes of the geranium leaves and rosemary lend a
sharpness to the overall aroma.*

ROSE AND
GARDEN-FLOWER POTPOURRI

2 cups rose petals and blooms
2 cups mixed garden flowers
1oz lavender
2oz mixed sweet herbs
1oz orris root powder
2 level teaspoons cinnamon powder
½ teaspoon whole cloves
2 star anise
3 drops rose oil
2 drops carnation oil
2 drops lemon oil

*Roses and other garden flowers combine to create a fresh floral pot-
pourri lighter in bouquet than an all-rose mix.*

❧ ROSE AND MINT POTPOURRI ❧

1 quart rose petals and blooms
1oz mint leaves
1oz lavender
1oz orris root powder
½ teaspoon whole cloves
1 teaspoon cinnamon powder
½ teaspoon ground mace
3 drops rose oil
2 drops rosewood oil
1 drop lemon oil

*A sweet rose potpourri with the refreshing influence of mint. The
mint has a distinctive aroma that contrasts beautifully with the
delicate perfume of the rose petals.*

Sweet-scented herbs

*From delicate, sweet aromas to sharp, tangy scents, simple,
charming, rustic mixes can be made from sweet herbs — ideal for
pine kitchens and cottage living-rooms.*

The scents of different flowers are easily confused, but the fragrances of sweet herbs are immediately recognizable. Who could confuse lavender with thyme, or rosemary with mint? Even those who have never lived in the country can tell these herbs apart.

Most sweet herbs are culinary: the flavors appeal to the palate, as much as the scents do to the nose. Culinary herbs were grown in monastery gardens centuries ago; Elizabethans included them in knot gardens; and today most of us grow at least a handful of them.

The earliest potpourris contained sweet herbs such as lavender, rosemary, bergamot, thyme, marjoram, costmary, balm, and mint, but any sweet-smelling herb can be used, including Mediterranean herbs that have been introduced more recently. Use what is available from your garden or window box to add to a herbal potpourri.

Create lovely piquant potpourris using lemon verbena, lemon balm, lemon thyme, lemon-scented geranium leaves and other sweet herbs whose leaves have a sharp, citric tang. Make fresh, minty mixes with delicate, spicy undertones to keep the air intriguingly sweet in the kitchen. Include lavender in a sweet-herb potpourri to introduce a floral note, or rosemary, whose pungent perfume lends strength to the overall fragrance. All the sweet-herb mixes shown look better in simple china, pottery, or enamel dishes.

They are not mixes for the elegant drawing room but rather for the cottage sitting-room, country bedroom, or simple rustic kitchen or bathroom.

Flowers to decorate

*Orange and
lemon peel*

Lemon verbena

Scented geranium leaf

Nutmeg

Vanilla bean

Rosemary

Lavender

❧ LEMON MIX ❧

Meadowsweet

Thyme

Marjoram

2 cups lemon verbena
2 cups mixed scented geranium leaves,
thyme, southernwood, meadowsweet flowers,
and marjoram
2oz rosemary
1oz orris root powder
2 teaspoons cinnamon powder
½ teaspoon grated nutmeg
½ teaspoon whole cloves
¼ vanilla bean
1oz lavender
a few pieces of orange and lemon peel
3 drops lemon oil
3 drops lavender oil
yellow flowers to decorate

A lemon-scented mixture of green sweet herbs.

Cinnamon   *Orris root*

Cloves

Lavender oil   *Lemon oil*

Southernwood

EASY SWEET-HERB MIX

1 quart mixed sweet herbs
1oz lavender
1oz orris root powder
2 teaspoons cinnamon powder
½ teaspoon whole cloves
3 drops lavender oil
3 drops lemon oil
flowers to decorate

A lavendery, sweet-herb potpourri with a hint of lemon.

SPICY HERB MIX

1 quart mixed lemon verbena, lemon-scented mint,
elecampane leaves, bergamot, and basil
2oz scented geranium leaves
1oz lavender
1oz orris root powder
2 teaspoons cinnamon powder
½ teaspoon ground allspice
½ teaspoon grated nutmeg
½ teaspoon caraway seeds
3 drops bergamot oil
3 drops geranium oil
flowers to decorate

A rich, aromatic herb potpourri decorated formally.

❧ PEPPERMINT MIX ❧

2 cups peppermint leaves
2 cups mixed lemon-scented mint, thyme,
costmary, and sweet cicely leaves
2oz rosemary
1oz lavender
1oz orris root powder
½ teaspoon ground allspice
½ teaspoon whole cloves
½ teaspoon grated nutmeg
2 cinnamon sticks
2 drops peppermint oil
2 drops basil oil
1 drop lemon oil
flowers to decorate

*A charming potpourri with a spicy peppermint fragrance that
will keep the kitchen smelling deliciously fresh.*

Wildflower & herb mixes

*Gentle colors and delicate perfumes characterize pretty,
wildflower and herb mixes.*

Many wildflowers exude strong perfumes that belie their unremarkable appearance. Fleabane grows unnoticed in its chalky limestone bed, but, when crushed, its leaves and roots produce a spicy fragrance that you would not expect from such a dingy-looking plant. Push your way through flowering gorse bushes, and the coconut smell of the blossoms will fill the air. Sweet woodruff and sweet clover have no smell while growing, but pick a bunch to hang dry, and the aroma of coumarin, like new-mown hay, is released. The quiet herbs marjoram, pennyroyal, and thyme contain sharp essential oils in their foliage. You might well pass by a bed of wild watermint without noticing it unless you happened to crush the leaves underfoot, giving rise to a sweet, minty fragrance. Birch buds, oakmoss, ground ivy, and wild strawberry are some of the other unlikely aromatic plants that grow all around us. Most wildflower potpourris are simple mixes, whose soft fragrances reflect the flowers' gentle coloring. The mixes illustrated feature wildflowers common in England. It is an offence to uproot any wildflower and it is best to try to grow your own. If this is impossible, remember never to pick a flower growing alone and be sure that you know which plants are protected by law (see p.123). Sweet cicely, pungent horehound, elecampane, fleabane, and meadowsweet can all be grown in the garden, where their roots can be harvested. Scented wildflowers, such as honeysuckle, bluebells, violets, hawthorn, evening primroses, and winter heliotrope can also be grown there alongside pale primroses and cowslips, which, for many, have the fleeting, evocative scent of childhood. As wildflowers are generally rather pale it is a good idea to decorate a wildflower mix with colorful cultivated flowers to improve its appearance.

Flowers to decorate

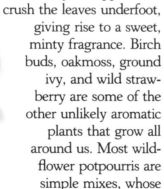

Mixed wild flowers

🌿 MIXED-FLOWER POTPOURRI 🌿

1 quart mixed wildflowers (excluding all
poisonous or acrid-smelling flowers)
2oz mixed pine needles, marjoram, sweet
cicely leaves, and meadowsweet leaves
1oz lavender
½ teaspoon juniper berries
1oz oakmoss
2 teaspoons ground mace
1oz orris root powder
2 teaspoons cinnamon powder
¼ vanilla bean
2 drops lavender oil
4 drops honeysuckle or violet oil
pink and yellow garden cinquefoils to decorate

A delicate, sweet-smelling potpourri.

Lavender

Vanilla bean

Juniper berries

Oakmoss

Mixed sweet herbs

Mace

Lavender oil

Honeysuckle oil

Cinnamon

Orris root

☙ WILD-MINT AND SWEETBRIER MIX ☙

2 cups mixed sweetbrier leaves and blossom
2 cups mixed wild mints
1oz marjoram
1oz lavender
1oz orris root powder
½ teaspoon whole cloves
½ teaspoon grated nutmeg
2 teaspoons cinnamon powder
1 drop lavender oil
1 drop peppermint oil
3 drops rose oil
flowers to decorate

A mixture with a delightful rose scent and a hint of mint.

☙ HEATHER- AND GORSE-FLOWER MIX ☙

1 quart mixed heather and gorse flowers
2oz oakmoss (or lavender)
1oz orris root powder
2 teaspoons cinnamon powder
½ teaspoon ground cloves
3 crushed cardamoms
2 drops lavender oil
2 drops rose oil
1 drop almond essence
flowers to decorate

A traditional floral fragrance with a hint of almond.

WOODRUFF MIX

1 quart mixed flowers, comprising three or more of the
following: honeysuckle, burnet rose, gorse, elder flower, lily-of-
the-valley, sweet violet, fleabane, and St. John's wort
2oz woodruff
2oz melilot (or another 2oz woodruff)
1oz costmary
1oz orris root powder
2 teaspoons ground mace

1 crushed tonka bean
½ teaspoon grated nutmeg
½ teaspoon ground allspice
3 drops rose, violet or lily-of-the-valley oil
3 drops lavender oil
flowers to decorate

*A rich and slightly musky floral potpourri. This mix of yellows,
pinks, and greens also looks very effective in a small wooden bowl o
unsophisticated wicker basket.*

Traditional fragrances

*These traditional mixes contain flowers, herbs, fixatives, and
spices used by the seventeenth- and eighteenth-century mistresses
of the household in the still-room.*

In Europe, as early as the sixteenth century, aromatic gums, resins, oils, spices, and woods were available to the perfumer and housewife. Specialist markets offered a great variety of imported and native aromatics for sale, and one can imagine the intriguing fragrances that wafted through the air. The mistress of the still-room (see p. 8) grew many of her own scented flowers, leaves, and roots, and traveling pedlars sold aromatics from the eastern Mediterranean and the Orient. Carnations, honeysuckle, violets, clove pinks, jonquils, mock orange blossom, and, of course, roses were among the scented flowers that she would have used. The old centifolia and damask roses retain a strong yet elusive perfume when dried and have always played an important role in the making of potpourri.

Although some old recipes do call for ingredients that are unobtainable now, you can still make potpourris that are similar to the early mixes. Frankincense, myrrh, and dried citrus peel were favorites then and are still readily available. The traditional mixes shown here yield the rich and aromatic perfumes common to many of the old recipes. They look beautiful displayed in china dishes, or elegant, pierced-lid potpourri jars.

Flowers to decorate

Lavender

Rose oil

Cedarwood oil

Rosemary oil

Rosemary

ROSE AND OAKMOSS POTPOURRI

1 quart mixed rose petals, buds, and blooms
2oz oakmoss
1oz rosemary
1oz lavender
1oz orris root powder
½oz marjoram
1oz cedarwood chips
¼ vanilla bean
2 drops rose oil
2 drops cedarwood oil
2 drops rosemary oil
flowers to decorate

The rich perfumes of roses and cedarwood pervade this mixture.

Marjoram

Oakmoss

Orris root

*Rose petals,
buds, and blooms*

Vanilla bean

Cedarwood

OLD-FASHIONED
MIXED-FLOWER POTPOURRI

1 quart mixed flowers from the following: rose, honeysuckle,
violet, pink, larkspur, lemon verbena, bachelor's button,
and wallflower
2oz mixed sweet herbs
1oz lavender
1oz orris root powder
1oz fine-ground gum benzoin
½ teaspoon whole cloves
½ teaspoon ground allspice
½ cinnamon stick
2 drops rose oil
2 drops carnation oil
1 drop lemon oil
1 drop frankincense oil
flowers to decorate

*A mixture of scented flowers and sweet herbs lends a rich, flowery
fragrance to this old-fashioned potpourri.*

SWEET-HERB AND ROSE-BUD POTPOURRI

2 cups rose petals and buds
2 cups mixed bergamot, sweet cicely leaves, marjoram, lemon
verbena, bay leaves,
and angelica leaves
1oz lavender
1oz orris root powder
2 teaspoons cinnamon powder
½ teaspoon angelica seeds
½ teaspoon whole cloves
½ teaspoon ground mace
¼ teaspoon grated nutmeg
3 drops rose oil
2 drops bergamot oil
1 drop frankincense oil
flowers to decorate

*The herbs and rose petals, together with a hint of frankincense,
make this potpourri richly aromatic.*

PRETTY VICTORIAN POTPOURRI

2 cups mixed pink, mauve, or cream, scented material from
the following: rose buds, violet, pink, chamomile flowers,
and heliotrope
2 cups mixed thyme, rosemary, myrtle, sweet cicely leaves,
and bergamot
1oz lavender
1oz orris root powder
1oz fine-ground gum benzoin
½ cinnamon stick
½ teaspoon whole cloves
½ teaspoon ground allspice
2 drops rose oil
2 drops lavender oil
2 drops lemon oil
pink and mauve flowers to decorate

*The prettiest, nostalgic Victorian potpourri with the sweet smell of
old-fashioned flowers.*

Seasonal scents

Although potpourris can be made all the year round, if you choose plant material from each season and create four separate potpourris, each seasonal mix will look and smell quite different.

The contents of a potpourri will reflect the season in which the flowers were gathered. A sensual winter mix has a different appearance and scent from a lavish summer potpourri; while a fragile spring mix contrasts strongly with a flamboyant autumn one.

The winter garden contains a surprising range of interesting scented material for gathering: scented evergreen leaves; the perfumed flowers of daphne, winter heliotrope, and water hawthorn; a few sweet-smelling herbs, such as rosemary and thyme; and scented woods, such as pine.

Spring poses no problems for the flower gatherer, for so many of the early flowers are scented. Jonquil, particularly the 'Soleil d'Or' variety, has the most stunning perfume of any flower I know. Most of the scents of flowers that bloom at this time of year are delicate and sweet, and spring potpourris reflect this bias.

Summer mixes are as varied and robust as summer blossoms. This is the time to experiment: mix colors, textures, shapes, and perfumes. Try combining "honeyed" roses, blue and pink larkspurs, blue bachelor's buttons, green angelica umbels, and bergamot.

Autumn calls for more ingenuity. Use the late-summer flowers as well as the true autumn blooms, and introduce berries, avoiding the poisonous ones (see p.123) to your mixes. They will add texture, interest, and variety to the fiery colors of the season.

Choose a container that is sympathetic to the character of each seasonal mix. To achieve a delightful rustic effect, I like to place my summer harvest of flowers in an old, lidded basket; winter browns look lovely in blue bowls; the reds, yellows, and oranges of autumn material look attractive displayed in a red enamel bowl; while the delicate flowers of spring require a fragile-looking dish to complement their charm fully, perhaps a white porcelain or a bone-china bowl.

Rosewood oil

Bergamot oil

Lavender oil

Mixed berries and cones

Orris root

Coriander

Star anise

Mixed sweet herbs

Cinnamon

Lavender

Mixed autumn flowers

AUTUMN POT POURRI

1 quart mixed autumn flowers in shades of pink, orange, yellow, and red
2oz mixed marjoram, elecampane leaves, bergamot leaves, and flowers
2oz lavender
1 cinnamon stick
1 star anise
1oz orris root powder
1 teaspoon coriander
2oz mixed rowan berries, alder cones, *Rosa moyesii* hips and *Rosa rugosa* hips
2 drops lavender oil
2 drops rosewood oil
2 drops bergamot oil

A striking mixture with a warm, sweet fragrance.

❧ WINTER POTPOURRI ❧

1 quart mixed alder cones, pine cones, pine needles, juniper
tips, and scented conifer tips
2oz mixed scented evergreen leaves, comprising: myrtle, bay,
eucalyptus, and box
1oz fine-ground gum benzoin
1oz lavender
2 teaspoons cinnamon powder
½ teaspoon whole cloves
½ vanilla bean
2 drops lavender oil
2 drops pine oil
2 drops lemon oil
'De Caen' anemones to decorate
N.B. Pine cones may be further scented by painting their
centers with pine oil.

*A sharp, spicy potpourri. The browns and greens of this strongly
scented mix are considerably enlivened by the luscious reds and
blues of the 'De Caen' anemones.*

❧ SPRING POTPOURRI ❧

1 quart mixed flowers, comprising four of the following:
jonquil, hyacinth, grape hyacinth, bluebell, violet, lily-of-the-
valley, wallflower, and lilac
2oz mixed herbs, comprising: bog myrtle,
crumbled bay, and chopped eucalyptus
1oz lavender
1oz orris root powder
2 teaspoons cinnamon powder
½ teaspoon coriander
4 drops jonquil oil
2 drops lavender oil
flowers to decorate

A fresh, flowery potpourri.

❧ SUMMER POTPOURRI ❧

1 quart mixed summer flowers
2oz mixed southernwood and mint
1oz lavender
1oz fine-ground gum benzoin
2 teaspoons cinnamon powder
½ teaspoon ground allspice
1 teaspoon sweet cicely seeds (optional)
1 teaspoon angelica seeds (optional)
2 drops rose oil
2 drops carnation oil
2 drops lavender oil
flowers to decorate

The profusion of flowers in summer makes this a colorful mix.

Country-garden charm

Pretty mixes of old-fashioned, country-garden flowers make refined and gentle potpourris. Cultivated for good reasons, every charming country-garden plant tells an intriguing story.

Cowslips, honeysuckle, cabbage roses, marigolds, lilies-of-the valley, pinks, and primroses: these are just a few of the scented flowers grown in the country garden. Add to these the perfumed rambler roses and jasmine, which clamber up walls and scramble over fences, and the sweet herbs, such as thyme, marjoram, rosemary, lavender, mint, woodruff, and elecampane, and you begin to appreciate the enormous diversity and potency of the scents that can abound in a country garden. The grower may have transplanted many of these plants from the wild. Some originally had medicinal purposes; others enhanced the flavor of food; and many perfumed the home, linen, and person.

Scented plants were grown indoors too; pots of pretty garden flowers crammed the kitchen windowsill.

The ingredients of a country-garden potpourri depend on what is available in the garden. Experiment with different mixes of any sweet-scented flowers, foliage, and roots until you discover the perfume and color combinations that please you most. Display them in unassuming wooden bowls or prettily decorated bone china dishes, jars, and lidded containers. An old pine washstand with its washbowl filled with potpourri looks charming, as does a copper saucepan or a humble soap dish brimful of fragrant flowers. In fact, any container with rustic charm will display these delicate potpourris to good effect.

❧ COUNTRY-GARDEN MIX ❧

2 cups mixed garden flowers
2 cups mixed southernwood, lemon balm, rosemary, and elecampane leaves
1oz lavender
1oz crushed bay leaf
peel of an orange
2oz orris root powder
2 teaspoons cinnamon powder
½ teaspoon ground cloves
½ teaspoon ground allspice
6 drops essential oil derived from one of the following:
lily-of-the-valley, honeysuckle, rose, jasmine, heliotrope, violet
flowers to decorate

Pretty old-fashioned flowers and sweet herbs mixed together make a light and sweet-scented potpourri.

Lavender

Mixed sweet herbs

Orange peel

Allspice

Orris root

Bay leaf

Mixed garden flowers and rose leaves

Rose oil

Cinnamon

Cloves

MARIGOLD, LEMON, AND MINT MIX

2 cups mixed marigold and chamomile flowers
2 cups mixed lemon balm and mint
2oz lavender
1oz rosemary
1oz orris root powder
½ cinnamon stick
1 strip lemon peel
½ teaspoon whole cloves
½ teaspoon grated nutmeg
3 drops geranium oil
2 drops lemon oil
1 drop peppermint oil
flowers to decorate (parsley, *Anaphalis* and blue larkspur)

*A sharp, fresh potpourri. The bold orange of the marigold flowers
makes this mix quite vibrant.*

FRAGRANT-ROOT POTPOURRI

2 cups mixed, chopped root, comprising at least three of the
following: geranium, roseroot, angelica, elecampane, sweet flag,
sweet cicely, and wood avens
1oz lavender
1oz orris root powder
½ teaspoon whole cloves
½ teaspoon ground allspice
2 teaspoons ground mace
1oz quassia chips
peel of a lime
4 drops rose oil
2 drops sandalwood oil
mock orange flowers to decorate

*A different style of potpourri with a refined and musky perfume
and highly textural appearance.*

❧ HERB AND LAVENDER MIX ❧

1 quart mixed woodruff,
rosemary, bergamot, and
elecampane leaves
2½oz lavender
1oz orris root powder
½ cinnamon stick
½ teaspoon ground cloves
½ teaspoon grated nutmeg
3 drops lavender oil
3 drops bergamot oil
flowers to decorate

*A soft and sweet-smelling potpourri that looks just right in an
unobtrusive rustic basket.*

Colorful combinations

Exquisite floral tapestries can be created with the flowers that are used in potpourri however limited the colors of the petals and blooms that are included.

Potpourri created from flowers of varying hues of the same color can be both interesting and pretty to look at, for, while the petals associate closely in color, their forms and textures provide considerable diversity. Flower textures vary enormously: petals may resemble chenille, velvet, crêpe, or satin; tiny umbels of flowers dry to scraps of knobbly lace; and panicles of small blooms and buds shrink to stitcheries of French and bullion knots. Arranged among herb leaves they have the tactile quality of rich embroidery.

The blues and purples, pinks and mauves, whites and creams, and yellows and oranges of the several kinds of potpourri displayed on the following three pages are just a few of the color combinations that can be made. Deep maroon and bright red rose petals mixed with scarlet cinquefoils and geraniums, red lychnis, tulip petals, and crimson fuchsias also make a stunning combination. Green flower mixes look exquisite and unusual: try combining the green flutes of *Nicotiana langsdorfii*, fragrant green *Tellima* bells, *Helleborus corsicus* and *H. lividus*, the perfumed green rose, and perhaps some green flowers from a fading hydrangea head for a beguiling mixture.

Blue flowers are scarcer than purple ones; yellow and orange flowers are prolific; white ones are more common than you would imagine; reds abound, as do pink and mauve blooms. Of all the flowers that can be used in potpourri, larkspurs yield the widest range of colors; they also retain their color well when dried.

Potpourri can be displayed in all sorts of containers, and part of the fun is searching for a dish that will either complement or offset the flowers. I prefer to use a bowl whose color is in the same range as the flowers. For instance, blue flowers look charming in Delft and willow pattern bowls, while white flowers have a quiet charm in a cool white bowl, or even an old china jelly mold.

Carnation oil Patchouli oil Rosemary oil

Cumin seeds

Mixed blooms

Mixed gray-leaved sweet herbs

Rosemary

Cardamoms

Star anise

Orris root Caraway seeds

PINK AND MAUVE MIX

1 quart petals and blooms in shades of pink and mauve
2oz mixed gray-leaved sweet herbs
1oz rosemary
1oz orris root powder
2 crushed cardamoms
½ teaspoon cumin seeds
2 star anise
½ teaspoon caraway seeds
4 drops carnation oil
2 drops rosemary oil
1 drop patchouli oil

This recipe uses a mixture of pretty pink flowers and gray-leaved sweet herbs. The essential oils and spices give the mix an elusively rich floral fragrance.

❦ YELLOW AND ORANGE MIX ❦

1 quart petals and blooms in shades of yellow
and orange
2oz mixed sweet herbs
1oz orris root powder
1oz lavender
2 teaspoons cinnamon powder
½ teaspoon grated nutmeg
½ teaspoon whole cloves
a few pieces lemon and orange peel
3 drops lemon oil
3 drops geranium oil

*Sweet-smelling herbs and yellow and orange flowers in a piquant,
lemony potpourri.*

WHITE AND CREAM MIX

1 quart petals and blooms in shades of
white and cream
2oz mixed sweet herbs
1oz rosemary
1oz orris root powder
2 teaspoons fine-ground gum benzoin
3 crushed cardamoms
½ teaspoon whole cloves
2 drops geranium oil
2 drops rosewood oil
1 drop lemon oil

*This unusual mixture of white flowers and herbs has a
charming, lingering sweet smell.*

BLUE AND MAUVE MIX

1 quart petals and blooms in shades of blue and mauve
2oz mixed gray-leaved sweet herbs
1oz lavender
1oz orris root powder
½ teaspoon whole cloves
½ teaspoon ground allspice
3 blades ground mace
3 drops lavender oil
2 drops bergamot oil

*Delft-blue flowers mixed with gray-leaved sweet herbs make a
charming potpourri with a lavender fragrance.*

A sense of occasion

*Potpourris for celebrations and special occasions range from
pretty, subtler, rose-scented mixes to stunning, exciting
combinations of color and texture.*

Potpourri makes a charming keepsake of celebrations where flowers play an important part, such as weddings, christenings, and birthdays. The blossoms from a bouquet can be easily dried and mixed with the ingredients of a potpourri to create a pretty reminder of the happy occasion that it celebrated. To complete such an ornamental mix, dry a few special flowers in a desiccant and decorate the top of the potpourri with the perfectly preserved blossoms. If you are using the flowers from a wedding bouquet, spray silver paint over a few of the flowers and scatter them over the top of the mixture to lend it a romantic luster. Add some traditional herbs as well: a few sprigs of basil for love, or marjoram for happiness.

For highly ornamental mixes, combine flowers of contrasting colors, such as green angelica flowers and dusky magenta roses, papery white hydrangeas and brown scented barks. Or spray faded hydrangea flowers metallic blue, green, and purple, and add them to a potpourri of blue and pink flowers to create a peacock mix in dazzling Islamic colors (see p. 43). Do not worry if the flowers you wish to use have no perfume of their own – simply add a scent of your choice in the form of an essential oil and spices. Be as daring with the container as with the flowers to create a highly decorative whole.

PEACOCK POTPOURRI

1 quart mixed flowers of blue, purple, and pink
2oz mixed sweet herbs
1oz lavender
1oz orris root powder
2 teaspoons cinnamon powder
½ teaspoon whole cloves
1 crushed tonka bean
1 star anise
2 drops sandalwood oil
2 drops rosewood oil
2 drops jasmine oil
metallic blue-, mauve-, and green-sprayed flowers to decorate

*Blue, purple, and mauve flowers combine with the dark green of
the mixed sweet herbs to provide an exotically perfumed potpourri.*

Star anise

Tonka bean

Cloves

Lavender

Mixed sweet herbs

Flowers to decorate

Mixed flowers

Sandalwood oil   Rosewood oil   Jasmine oil

Orris root

Cinnamon

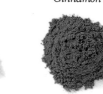

RED AND WHITE POTPOURRI

1 quart red rose petals and blooms, and any pretty white
flowers
2oz mixed sweet herbs
1oz rosemary
1oz orris root powder
½ teaspoon whole cloves
1 teaspoon crushed cassia
3 teaspoons ground mace
3 drops rose oil
2 drops rosemary oil
1 drop rosewood oil

*A slightly spicy, rose-scented blend of mixed white flowers and
bright red rose petals and blooms.*

ELIZABETHAN POTPOURRI

1 quart mixed red, blue, purple, brown, and
yellow flowers
2oz mixed chopped sweet flag
leaves, elecampane leaves, sweet cicely leaves, angelica
leaves, and bergamot
1oz rosemary
1oz orris root powder
1oz sandalwood raspings
½ teaspoon whole cloves
½ teaspoon grated nutmeg
2 drops sandalwood oil
2 drops bergamot oil
2 drops rose oil
1 drop frankincense oil
gilded achillea flowers to decorate

A richly colored and perfumed "still-room" potpourri.

WEDDING POTPOURRI

1 quart mixed white and pink rose petals, orange blossom,
myrtle flowers, white hydrangea flowers, pink rose buds, and
any flowers from the bridal bouquet
2oz mixed myrtle leaves, basil, rose leaves, and marjoram
1oz rosemary
1oz fine-ground gum benzoin
1oz orris root powder
1 crushed cardamom
1 teaspoon crushed cassia
3 drops rose oil
2 drops lavender oil
1 drop patchouli oil
silver-sprayed flowers to decorate

*Traditional herbs of love, fidelity and happiness are here mixed
with some of the predominantly pink and white flowers from a
traditional wedding bouquet.*

Exotic influences

*Whether discreet, scented wood mixes, heady flower combinations,
or sweetly scented fruits and spices, all these recipes have a hint of the exotic.*

Many of the spices, oils, scented woods and flowers, gums, resins, and even herbs that are used in potpourri come from as far afield as the eastern Mediterranean and the Orient. The sharp-scented dried peel of lemons, oranges, and limes has been used for centuries, and more recently citrus fruits, such as the aptly named ugli fruit, the diminutive kumquat, and the pretty, pink-skinned grapefruit, have become available. Dried tropical fruits and vegetables that add color and texture but not scent to a mix include translucent slices of kiwi fruit, intriguing rosettes of star fruit, and even baby sweetcorn.

Exotic flowers that are ideal for potpourri include jasmine, lilies, orange blossom, mimosa, and narcissi. Mixed with pungent spices, the smallest amount of patchouli or ilang-ilang oil, and a few drops of a tropical flower oil, these flowers make heady and exotic potpourris. It is best to display such mixes in large, open rooms, where their fragrance will not become intrusive or overpowering.

For those who do not like floral perfumes, many of the exotic scented woods make intriguing spiced, musky-smelling potpourris. Sandalwood and cedarwood shavings, cinnamon sticks, logwood chips, balsam poplar buds, agar, wood, and cassia are all quite easy ingredients to obtain.

I like to see woody mixes displayed in plain bowls, while fruit potpourris are best arranged in large, roomy containers where the lovely colors and shapes can be seen to best advantage. Recipes that include tropical flowers and perfumes look best in Chinese or Japanese containers.

🌿 EXOTIC WOOD MIX 🌿

1 quart mixed woods, comprising three or four of the following: sandalwood shavings, cinnamon stick, balsam poplar buds, logwood chips, cedarwood shavings, agar wood shavings, white cinnamon, and cassia
2oz lavender
1 teaspoon fine-ground gum olibanum
4 crushed cardamoms
½ teaspoon ground cloves
½ teaspoon of the peel of each of the following: orange, lemon, and lime
1oz orris root powder
2 teaspoons cinnamon powder
1 teaspoon ground allspice
1 vanilla bean
2 drops cedarwood oil
2 drops lavender oil
2 drops ilang-ilang oil
flowers to decorate

An interesting, oriental, mixed-wood potpourri.

Flowers and hips for decoration

Mixed woods

Orange peel

Cloves

Lavender

Vanilla bean

Orris root

Gum olibanum

Ilang-ilang oil   *Cedarwood oil*   *Lavender oil*

Cinnamon

Cardamoms

Allspice

❧ CITRUS FRUIT POTPOURRI ❧

1 quart mixed lime, lemon, orange, tangerine,
and grapefruit peel
2oz eucalyptus leaves
1oz orris root powder
2 cinnamon sticks

1 teaspoon coriander
½ teaspoon grated nutmeg
2 crushed tonka beans
½ teaspoon whole cloves
4 drops lemon oil
2 drops bergamot oil
kumquats and yellow flowers to decorate

A visually stunning, tangy-scented potpourri.

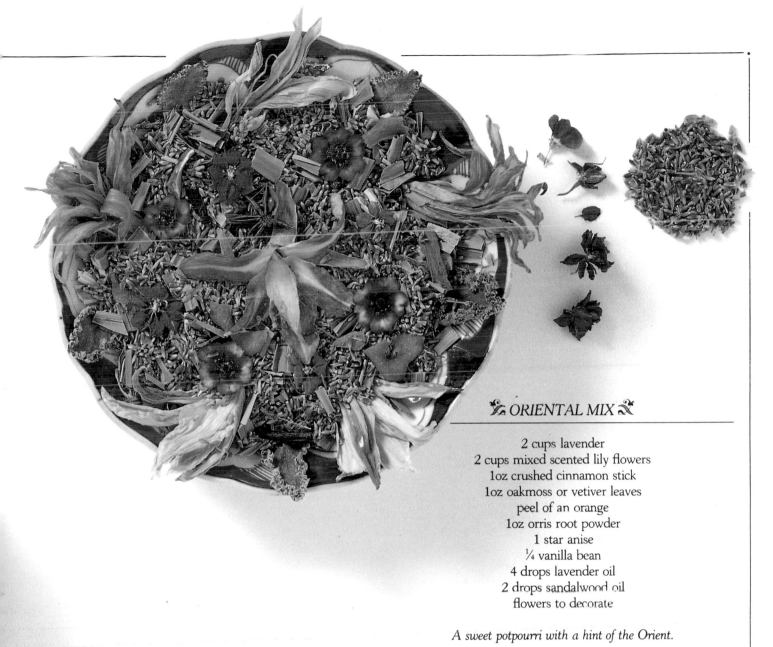

✣ ORIENTAL MIX ✣

2 cups lavender
2 cups mixed scented lily flowers
1oz crushed cinnamon stick
1oz oakmoss or vetiver leaves
peel of an orange
1oz orris root powder
1 star anise
¼ vanilla bean
4 drops lavender oil
2 drops sandalwood oil
flowers to decorate

A sweet potpourri with a hint of the Orient.

✣ TURKISH POTPOURRI ✣

1 quart mixed rose petals and buds, and jasmine and
orange blossom
2oz mixed patchouli leaves, scented geranium leaves,
basil, and marjoram
1oz lavender
peel of an orange
1oz cedarwood shavings
1oz fine-ground gum benzoin
2 cinnamon sticks
1 teaspoon whole cloves
½ teaspoon grated nutmeg
2 drops lavender oil
2 drops rose oil
1 drop lemon oil
1 drop patchouli oil
flowers to decorate

*A slightly citric blend with a rich and heavy fragrance. This heady
potpourri has a distinctly eastern Mediterranean flavor.*

Heady aromas

Potpourris made using the moist method have a deliciously rich perfume. Although not quite as simple to make as dry potpourris, their fragrance is significantly more enduring.

The perfume of a moist potpourri is quite different from that of a dry one, for, although it contains the shadowy fragrance of the scented flowers that have been used, the scent has much more substance. The long curing process, during which brandy and sugar have probably been added, results in an intensely sweet, much richer perfume. The moist method (see p. 98) is the oldest and most traditional method of making potpourri and is perhaps the most rewarding. Time is less important when making a moist recipe: you can add the partially dried petals to the preserving jar as and when they become available, and you can effect the final mixing whenever you like: it will improve with age.

Traditionally, rose petals are used in moist mixes, but any sweetly scented flowers and leaves are suitable. Whichever petals you choose, they will not look particularly attractive when the moist potpourri mixture has cured. So if you wish to display the deliciously scented "stock-pot" petals and other added ingredients that emerge from the curing container, in an open bowl, decorate the top with some pretty dried flowers to give the mix an attractive appearance. The more traditional way of using a moist mix is to place it in a special potpourri jar with a perforated lid, or in a pretty, covered container, which you can open whenever you wish to do so. In this way, the inviting perfume will last for several years.

Lavender oil   *Geranium oil*

Orange peel

Crumbled and cured rose petals

Flowers to decorate

Cloves

Bay leaf

Marjoram

Mixed herbs

❧ LAVENDER MIX ❧

Orris root

1 quart crumbled stock-pot petals
2oz lavender
1oz marjoram
2oz mixed rosemary, thyme,
and lemon balm
3 crumbled bay leaves
1 teaspoon grated orange peel
1oz orris root powder
½ teaspoon cinnamon powder
½ teaspoon ground cloves
½ teaspoon grated nutmeg
2 drops lavender oil
3 drops rose geranium oil
flowers to decorate if required

Lavender

Nutmeg

Cinnamon

A pungent floral moist potpourri with a hint of citrus.

❧ SWEET FLORAL POTPOURRI ❧

1 quart crumbled stock-pot petals
1oz lavender
½oz fine-ground gum benzoin
1oz orris root powder
½ chopped vanilla bean
1 teaspoon crushed cardamom
½ teaspoon ground cloves

½ teaspoon grated nutmeg
1 drop frankincense oil
2 drops lavender oil
3 drops rose oil
flowers to decorate if required

A rich and sweet, flowery potpourri. Decorate the mix with flowers or keep in a lidded container. Here, dried rich-red and pink rose and cinquefoil flowers empathize with the translucent pink dish.

ROSE, MOCK ORANGE, ❧ AND CARNATION MIX ❧

1 quart mixed fresh rose petals, fresh mock orange blossom,
and fresh clove carnation or pink flowers
2oz mixed fresh mint, fresh marjoram, and
fresh rosemary
2oz lavender
4 bay leaves
1oz cinnamon powder
½ teaspoon ground cloves
lavender water (sprinkling)
brandy (sprinkling)
½oz fine ground gum benzoin
¼ teaspoon grated nutmeg
½oz orris root powder
4oz coarse salt (not table salt)

*An ancient recipe for a moist potpourri, which is made differently
from other moist mixes in that all the ingredients are mixed
together and layered in a jar with the salt, brandy, and lavender
water. The jar is then sealed and the contents left to cure for two
months, stirring daily. This tall glass jar was layered with dried
flowers, herbs, and spices, and a muslin bag filled with the matured
potpourri was buried inside.*

❧ LEMON MIX ❧

1 quart crumbled stock-pot petals
1oz lavender
2oz mixed lemon balm and lemon verbena
1oz lemon-scented geranium leaves
1oz rosemary
crushed peel of ¼ lemon
1oz orris root powder
½ teaspoon cinnamon powder
½ teaspoon ground cloves
3 drops lemon oil
2 drops rose oil
1 drop lavender oil
flowers to decorate if required

*A very lemony and piquant potpourri. Here, dried rose petals and
blooms decorate the mix when the lid is removed.*

PIQUANT FLORAL MIX

1 quart crumbled stock-pot petals
2oz rose geranium leaves
1oz lavender
1oz orris root powder
dried rind of ½ lemon
1 crushed tonka bean
½ teaspoon ground allspice
½ teaspoon grated nutmeg
2 drops lavender oil
2 drops rose geranium oil
2 drops lemon oil

Deliciously scented rose geranium leaves add a sharpness to this piquant floral recipe, which is further enhanced by a subtle hint of lemon.

BERGAMOT AND ROSE MIX

1 quart crumbled stock-pot petals
2oz bergamot leaves
1oz lavender
1oz fine-ground gum benzoin

1 star anise
½ teaspoon cinnamon powder
½ teaspoon whole cloves
1 drop patchouli oil
3 drops bergamot oil
3 drops rose oil

An old recipe using the traditional fragrances of roses and bergamot leaves. The three oils used give the mix a lovely pungent aroma.

SWEET COUNTRY MIX

1 quart crumbled stock-pot petals
2oz myrtle leaves
1oz lavender
1oz orris root powder
½ teaspoon whole cloves
½ teaspoon coriander
½ vanilla bean
5 drops rose oil

The unusual fragrance of myrtle leaves makes this potpourri especially distinctive.

CHAPTER TWO

Fragrance in Disguise

There are many delightful ways in which potpourri can be used to perfume a host of accessories for the home. Cushions, nightdress and handkerchief cases, sachets, tussie mussies, flower baskets, soaps, and even bath water can all be perfumed with potpourri. Perfume a pillow with a sleep-inducing potpourri and, even if you don't fall asleep immediately, what could be nicer than resting your head on a cushion that imparts the shadowy smell of lavender and hops; scented cushions can be appliquéd with scraps of lace and embroidered, or made from pretty floral fabrics; sachets can be lacy, transparent, flowery, or embroidered, and made in any shape that appeals to you. Add to the fragrance of tussie mussies and flower baskets by including little net balls of potpourri in the arrangements. In the bathroom, store soaps in pretty glass jars or dishes of potpourri, so that they absorb the fragrance, and place special mixes in muslin bags and use them to perfume the bath water.

Materials & equipment

An intriguing cornucopia of scented accessories can be made using fragrant plant materials in conjunction with lace and cotton, citrus fruits, other flowers, or soaps.

Nothing that I suggest making in this chapter is difficult and none of the materials hard to find. Choose pretty fabrics and threads for sachets and cushions, and, if possible, dye your own decorative lace to match; hang citrus pomanders with complementary ribbons; finish off posies with color-washed paper doilies; and match the colors of a potpourri to the soaps that sit in it. If you are daunted by embroidery, appliqué pretty scraps of material to a cushion, sachet, or nightie case instead, or sew on pretty beads and sequins for a highly decorative finish.

Rewarding to make, and wonderful presents to give and receive, you will find fragrant, decorative ideas for every room in the house: cushions for sitting rooms, dining rooms, and kitchens; scent pillows and nightie cases for bedrooms; pomanders for hanging anywhere; tussie mussies, baskets, and bouquets of flowers for tables, shelves, and windowsills; little sachets that can be popped in drawers and cupboards; and herb sachets for the bath water. You will need only the equipment shown on these two pages, plus your choice of fabrics and plant materials in order to make them. Our ancestors knew the importance of distributing these aromatics throughout their homes, and, once you have experienced the pleasures they bring, you will undoubtedly wish to turn your hand to such crafts as sewing or flower arranging so that you can fill your home with fragrant delights.

Sachets and pillows
Pillows, nightie cases, sachets, and coat hangers are just some of the delightful perfumed things to be made out of pretty cotton fabrics, silk, lace, or calico (pp. 58-71).

Lavender

Beads and sequins

Needlework scissors

Fabric and wadding

Pins

Needles

Sewing thread

Embroidery silks

Cords

Laces

Metal knitting needle

Orange

Plastic bag

Cinnamon

Orris root

Florist's medium-gauge wire

Doily

Basket

Reel wire

Rose wire

Pins

Ribbons

Cloves

Tape

Potpourri

Silk net

Dry florist's foam

Cinnamon stick

Decorated star anise

Florist's tape

Scissors

Dried rose bloom

Muslin

Rose petals, bloom, and leaf

Soap

Pomanders
Very little is needed to make these traditional aromatic citrus pomanders. Cloves and cinnamon powder can usually be found in the kitchen, and orris root powder can be bought in most health food shops. Decorate citrus pomanders with pretty velvet or satin ribbons tied in loops and bows at the top. Hang them at different heights at a window, or place several in a bowl or basket and display them on top of a table or windowsill (pp. 72-75).

Soaps and bath sachets
Perfumed soaps, fragrant bath sachets, and pretty pot-pourris can all be made for the bathroom. Make dainty flower mixes that reflect the colors in your bathroom, and display unperfumed soaps in potpourri, where they will absorb the fragrance. Sew muslin bath sachets of mixed herbs, and keep them in glass jars prettily decorated with pressed flowers (pp. 82-84).

Flower arrangements
The fragrance of pretty baskets, bouquets, and nosegays of flowers and herbs is enriched by the addition of wired spices and bundles of potpourri. Fill baskets with dry florist's foam to create a secure base in which to arrange the plant material. Surround tussie mussies with paper doilies for a little extra decoration (pp. 76-81).

Scented sachets

Used for centuries to perfume linens and clothes, scented sachets, or sweet bags, can be suspended in cupboards or laid flat in drawers to scent garments, sheets, and even paper.

Thousands of years ago the Greeks placed sprigs and leaves of aromatic herbs among their linen, realizing that some herbs had insecticidal properties, while others imparted a lingering sweet fragrance. In the Orient, patchouli leaves were used to protect beautiful Kashmir shawls and precious textiles from the ravages of insects. In Europe, as early as the sixteenth century, little bags of sweetly scented, and occasionally insect-repellent, flowers and herbs were placed among clothes, linen, and even books.

Often, the ingredients for sachets were ground into a powder to amalgamate fully the perfumes of the ingredients used, and to accommodate any bulky aromatic ingredients. Today, there is less need to grind the materials as we rely on essential oils to perfume a mix. I always make strongly scented mixes for placing in sachets, as each little bag contains only a small amount of potpourri.

Sweet bags can be designed to hang in cupboards and on coat hangers, suspended from beams and door knobs, fastened to chairs, placed in pillow slips, or stood on a bathroom shelf. Of course, moth- and insect-repellent mixes do not have a floral bias, and I would recommend tansy, southernwood, and rue for sachets made for this purpose.

MAKING A FLAT SACHET

1 Select a suitable fabric for the sachet – a light material made from natural fibers is ideal. With a pair of pinking shears, cut out two squares of fabric, 4 × 4 in. Cut a strip of lace 32 in. long. Pin the two fabric squares together.

2 Gather the lace until it is just over 16 in. long and sew it to three edges of the sachet, through both layers of fabric, leaving the fourth side free. Make up the sweet bag mix using the dry method (see p. 96). Fill the sachet with potpourri and sew the lace to the fourth side in the same way to close it.

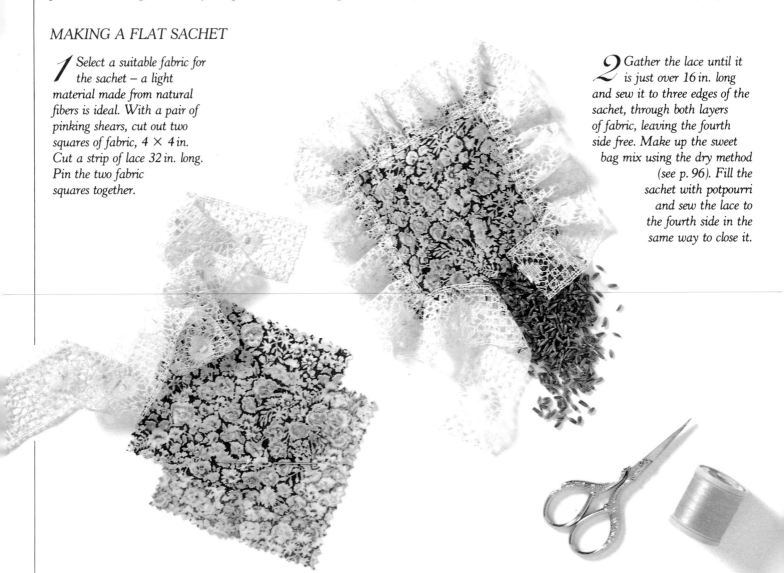

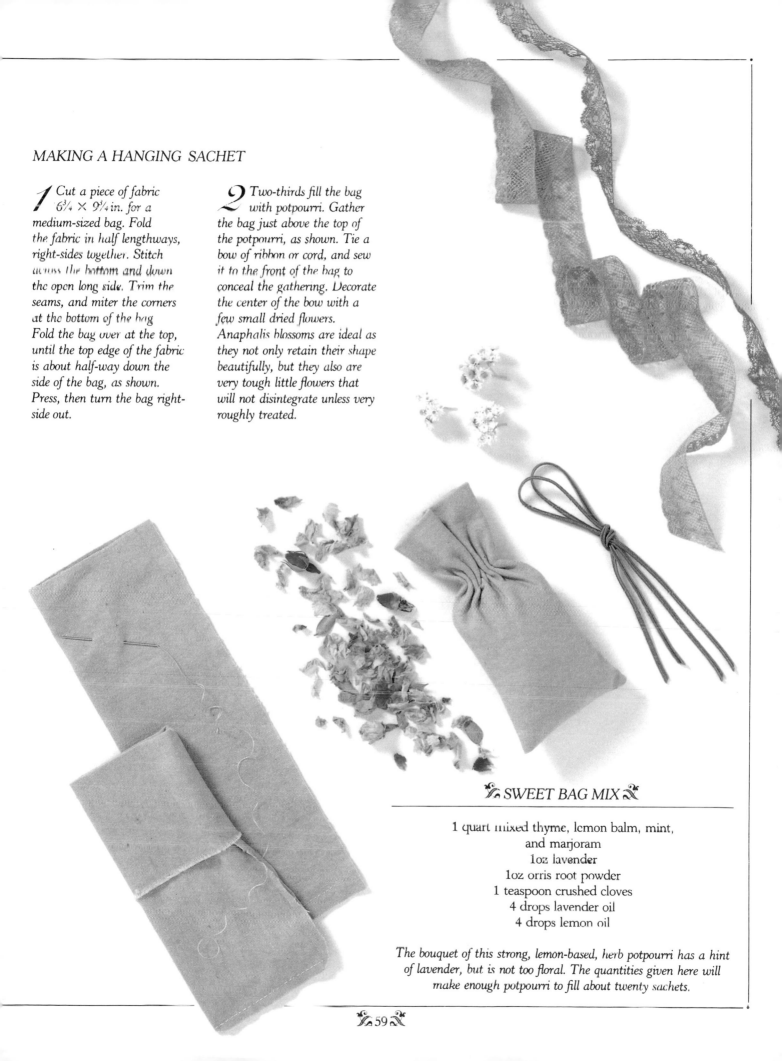

MAKING A HANGING SACHET

1 *Cut a piece of fabric 6¾ × 9¾ in. for a medium-sized bag. Fold the fabric in half lengthways, right-sides together. Stitch across the bottom and down the open long side. Trim the seams, and miter the corners at the bottom of the bag. Fold the bag over at the top, until the top edge of the fabric is about half-way down the side of the bag, as shown. Press, then turn the bag right-side out.*

2 *Two-thirds fill the bag with potpourri. Gather the bag just above the top of the potpourri, as shown. Tie a bow of ribbon or cord, and sew it to the front of the bag to conceal the gathering. Decorate the center of the bow with a few small dried flowers. Anaphalis blossoms are ideal as they not only retain their shape beautifully, but they also are very tough little flowers that will not disintegrate unless very roughly treated.*

✂ SWEET BAG MIX ✂

1 quart mixed thyme, lemon balm, mint, and marjoram
1oz lavender
1oz orris root powder
1 teaspoon crushed cloves
4 drops lavender oil
4 drops lemon oil

The bouquet of this strong, lemon-based, herb potpourri has a hint of lavender, but is not too floral. The quantities given here will make enough potpourri to fill about twenty sachets.

ROSY MIX

1 quart rose petals
1oz lavender
1oz orris root powder
1 teaspoon cinnamon powder
6 drops rose oil
2 drops lavender oil

A traditional and penetrating rose-petal potpourri, the fragrance is sweet and mildly spicy, and will probably appeal more to women than men. It fills the sachets at left.

WOODY MIX

1 quart sandalwood shavings
1oz bergamot leaves
1oz orris root powder
1 teaspoon ground cloves
4 drops sandalwood oil
4 drops bergamot oil

With a lingering and traditional masculine fragrance of sandalwood and sharp bergamot, these sachets (above) can be looped over wardrobe hangers and tucked among shirts.

Miniature sachets
Even the smallest snippets of lace, ribbon, or pretty material can be made into little bags, squares, or decorative shapes, and filled with potpourri. Decorate rose-petal sachets with tiny satin or pressed rose buds, and glue pressed flowers to the front of lace-trimmed sachets, before protecting them with fine net. Dye laces and ribbons in lovely muted colors appropriate to the colors of the mixes, and embroider or embellish some sachets with beads and sequins. Suspend them with pretty matching ribbons.

Pillows of herbs

That perfume is therapeutic and uplifting has been well known for centuries, and, as early as the sixteenth century, mattresses and pillows were stuffed with fragrant materials.

Scented grasses and woodruff, with perhaps the addition of lavender or rose petals, fresh pine foliage, scented flowering heather, hops, or even aromatic wood shavings have been commonly used in mattresses since time immemorial. Pillows were filled with similar mixes, although the plant material used was generally less bulky and more refined to ensure that the scent was not overwhelming. Soothing mixes of hops and lavender, herb mixtures, light floral combinations, and even spicy mixes, were commonly placed in what later became known as sleep pillows.

Herb pillows today range from simple sprigged cotton or patchwork cushions to highly decorative lace or embroidered ones. Whichever kind you decide to make, try dyeing the material yourself to obtain a pretty shade that suits the room in which the pillow will be placed. The lace and calico of the pink and blue hydrangea-colored embroidered cushions on pages 68 and 69 were home-dyed, and they would look delightful in a romantic bedroom. Scented pillows can also be made for chairs and sofas to perfume a room. Fill the pillows or cushions with a potpourri of your choice, remembering that almost everyone likes a light, fresh floral fragrance and that the perfume emanating from a pillow should not be overwhelming. Scented and embroidered commemorative cushions can be made to celebrate a wedding, birthday, or any other special occasion. Simply embroider the message, in stem stitch, on the upper side of the cushion to make a beautiful and very special gift.

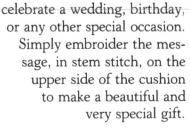

❧ SHARP ROSE MIX ❧

1 pint strongly fragrant rose petals
1 pint mixed lemon verbena, rosemary,
and woodruff
1oz lavender
1oz orris root powder
½ teaspoon crushed cloves
grated and dried rind of an orange
4 drops rose oil
4 drops bergamot oil

The herbs and bergamot oil sharpen the fragrance of the sweet, rosy perfume that emanates from this strong, piquant potpourri, ideal for pillows or sachets.

MAKING A SQUARE CUSHION

1 Take some cotton fabric of your choice and some synthetic wadding 4 oz weight. With a pair of sewing scissors, cut out two square pieces of fabric 8 × 8 in. Next, cut out six square pieces of wadding approximately 7 × 7 in. This will ensure that the cushion is pleasantly padded. Make up the sharp rose mix using the dry method (see p. 96). You will have enough of the distinctively perfumed potpourri to make four plump pillows.

2 To make the inner cushion, place the six squares of synthetic wadding one on top of the other. Using a tacking stitch, sew around three sides of the wadding, leaving the fourth side open. Ensure that all six pieces are joined together firmly. Spoon the potpourri into the middle of the pad of wadding until it is a plump cushion. Sew up the fourth side of the layers of wadding in the same way as the other three, to close the scented pad.

3 To make the pillow case, place the two pieces of fabric right-sides together, and machine stitch around three sides. Trim the seams and miter the corners. Turn the case right-side out and press. Insert the potpourri-filled pad into the case, easing it into the corners. Sew up the fourth side by hand, so that the stitching can be undone easily when you wish to wash the fabric or renew the potpourri packed inside the inner pad of the cushion.

❧ SOOTHING MIX ❧

1 pint violets
1 pint rose petals
1oz rosemary
1oz orris root powder
1 crushed tonka bean
½ chopped vanilla bean
dried peel of half a lemon
3 drops violet oil
2 drops rose oil
1 drop lemon oil

*This gentle, soothing, and quiet mix is ideal for a sleep pillow. It
has a musky floral fragrance with a hint of vanilla.*

RICH MIX

1 pint juniper tips or any other scented conifer tips
1 pint lemon verbena
1oz woodruff
1oz rosemary
1oz orris root powder
1 crushed tonka bean
2 drops pine oil
1 drop rosemary oil
2 drops lemon oil

*The inclusion of woodruff and rosemary in this lemon
and pine mix gives the potpourri a slightly deeper
note. There are no spicy overtones.*

Lace cushions
Dusky pink and blue tones, reminiscent of the colors of hydrangea flowers, were chosen for the fabric and thread of these pretty, hand-dyed calico and lace cushions, which are stuffed with a floral-scented potpourri. The embroidery was stitched in simple French and bullion knots.

Victorian-style cases
The exquisite perfumed calico nightie and hanky cases (far left) are easy to make: simply stuff an embroidered envelope shape with a thin potpourri-filled pad. To make a scented coat hanger, enclose a hanger in a tube of wadding filled with potpourri, then cover. The large, lace-trimmed cushion (above) is stuffed with hops and lavender.

Piquant pomanders

*Aromatic balls were made by the Ancient Greeks, although
citrus pomanders were not made until the sixteenth century.*

The first reference to pomanders as we understand them can be found in European medical literature of the thirteenth century, where an aromatic ball known as *pomum ambrae,* meaning "apple of amber," was said to be worn or carried to ward off disease. These early pomanders were apple-sized balls of aromatic materials, including fixatives such as ambergris, musk, civet, and castor, which were believed to possess disinfecting properties. The early Christians also used scented pomander beads as rosaries and, during the Renaissance, beautiful prayer beads of pearls and precious metals were coated in aromatic materials and encased in exquisite filigree. By the sixteenth century, decorative containers for larger pomanders, known as pouncet-boxes, were hung around the neck or waist, or carried, by the wealthy. The pierced china balls filled with aromatics that can be bought today, are descendants of these pouncet-boxes. Citrus fruits, studded with cloves and rolled in spices, are described in literature of the sixteenth century.

Today, the most popular pomanders are made from citrus fruits, ranging from pink and yellow grapefruits, through oranges and lemons, to small tangerines and limes. The scent of one of these pomanders is rather like a spiced citrus potpourri, but it varies according to the essential oils that have been added to the spice mixture in which the fruit is rolled or shaken. The prettiest of floral pomanders can also be made simply by covering balls of dried florist's foam with spices, and scented flowers and leaves. Try hanging pomanders in cupboards, from ceiling beams, or on varying lengths of ribbon at a window. They also look delightful placed in a basket.

MAKING A CITRUS POMANDER

1 Take a length of tape, slightly wider than the ribbon you intend using to decorate or suspend the citrus fruit. Pin the tape to the fruit – here an orange – encircling it and dividing the fruit in half. Pin another length of tape to the orange, dividing it roughly into quarters.

2 Using a thin metal knitting needle, and working on one quarter segment of the orange at a time, pierce holes about ¼ in. apart, from the top to the base of the orange, as shown. Work right up to the edges of the tape. Insert a clove in each hole.

❧ YOU WILL NEED ❧

Citrus fruit: grapefruit, orange, tangerine, ugli fruit,
clementine, lemon, or lime
Cloves
Spice mixture: a few drops of essential oil, such as lemon
verbena or bergamot, mixed with equal amounts of
cinnamon and orris root powder
Equipment: cotton tape, pins, metal knitting needle, and
greaseproof or tissue paper
Decoration: ribbons

3 Stick cloves in all four segments of the fruit. Make up as much of the spice mixture as required − 2 oz of spices will be enough to cover about six oranges. Place the spice mixture in a plastic bag. Remove the tape from the orange and put the orange in the bag. Seal the top, and shake vigorously. Wait for the spices to settle and then undo the bag and remove the orange, tapping it to remove excess spices. Wrap the pomander in greaseproof or tissue paper and put it in a warm, dry, dark spot, such as an airing cupboard. Leave for two to three weeks to cure.

4 During the curing process, the pomander will shrink slightly and become harder. Decorate it with brightly colored florist's ribbon or velvet, soft satin or embroidered ribbon. Wrap it around the pomander, covering the area where the tapes were placed originally.

Try laying a narrow ribbon over a wider one, and mixing the colors for an eye-catching effect. Tie a loop at the top by which to suspend the pomander, or make a flat bow on top if the pomander is to be displayed on a flat surface or in a dish.

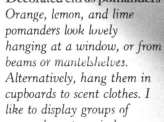

Decorated citrus pomanders
Orange, lemon, and lime pomanders look lovely hanging at a window, or from beams or mantelshelves. Alternatively, hang them in cupboards to scent clothes. I like to display groups of pomanders at a window. Large grapefruit pomanders are too heavy to hang and should be displayed on a shelf or table.

Basket of citrus pomanders
A rustic basket crammed with citrus pomanders, fresh kumquats, whole spices, and some bright yellow statice heads makes an intriguing display of aromatic materials. Made from grapefruits, oranges, lemons, and limes, the charm of these pomanders lies in their unadorned simplicity. The overall spicy aroma from a basket of mixed pomanders is delicious.

Flower pomanders
You can create the most exquisite hanging collages of flowers, herbs, and spices. Cover a ball of dry florist's foam with a rubber-based glue, and roll the ball in lavender: this will give you the scented base for the pomander. Glue any further decorative material on to the flower-ball carefully, piece by piece. Ornamentation can be rich and formal or as random and pretty as a typical country garden.

Scented flower arrangements

The perfume of a posy, bouquet, or basket of flowers can be enhanced by one or two fragrant sachets of potpourri.

Scented sachets, or balls, for flower arrangements are extremely quick and easy to make. Simply enclose potpourri in net to make a little ball, or bundle, and push it on to a length of medium-gauge florist's wire. Then incorporate the wired bundle into the flower arrangement. The potpourri will show through the net, so ensure that its colors blend with those of the flowers. For example, a little bundle of rose-petal potpourri will look delightful in the center of a posy of pink flowers; a basket of dried herbs will look and smell more delicious if little green bags of a herb-based potpourri are arranged among the foliage; and a lovely bouquet of richly colored dried flowers is even more attractive when perfumed with little net bundles of deep-red petals.

Tussie mussies, or little posies of scented and traditional herbs and flowers, can convey a message, according to the "meaning" of the herbs and flowers used in them. In the past their fragrance was believed to ward off the plague and other infectious diseases, so they were frequently carried as protection against ill health. Tussie mussies are easy to make: arrange the flowers around a little potpourri bundle and wire the stems together.

Try perfuming an arrangement of fir cones, berries, and dried conifer foliage with pine-scented, potpourri sachets, or perhaps musky sandalwood bundles. Alternatively, scent a flower arrangement with spices: bend a length of medium-gauge florist's wire over the center of a star anise or insert into a halved cinnamon stick or vanilla bean.

Flat tussie mussie
To make this little posy, cut 1¼ in. off the top of a medium-sized ball of dry florist's foam and glue flower heads, and tiny sprigs of herbs and foliage to it. Encircle a little bundle of rose-petal potpourri with roses, anaphalis, herbs, heather, sneezewort, queen-anne's lace, and ferns.

❧ YOU WILL NEED ❧

For the bundles: fine net, needle and thread, potpourri, and medium-gauge florist's wire
For spicy arrangements: star anise, cinnamon sticks, vanilla beans, dried flowers, medium-gauge florist's wire, sprays of dried herbs and foliage, dry florist's foam, and containers
For the posies: dried flowers, medium-gauge florist's wire, sprays of dried herbs and foliage, and paper doilies

MAKING A LAVENDER BUNDLE

1 Cut out a circle of cardboard about 3 in. in diameter. Place it on a piece of fine net and draw around it with a soft pencil. Cut the net along the penciled line, then, using a doubled cotton thread, sew around the entire edge of the net circle with running stitches. Gather the thread to make a little open container.

2 Using a teaspoon, carefully fill the net container almost to the top with lavender. Pull the gathering thread tight and knot securely. Push the tip of a length of medium-gauge florist's wire into the lavender bundle, through the base where the gathering has been secured. To secure the wire stem more firmly, bend the tip of the wire into a hook and push it through the top of the bundle.

Potpourri of varying scents and colors can be placed in such a sachet, depending on the scent and colors of the arrangement that you wish to perfume. A rose mix, an herb-based potpourri, or even a woody mix, all make lovely bundles, which always enhance the flower arrangements.

Wired perfumed material
All sorts of aromatic material can be used in a bouquet, tussie mussie, or flower basket, although some must first be wired. Break a stick of cinnamon (near left) or vanilla bean in half and push a length of medium-gauge wire through the center of each. Bend wire over a star anise (center left) and decorate the center with an anaphalis flower. Coat a tiny ball of dry florist's foam with glue, roll it in aromatic seeds, and push it on to a wire stem.

Tiny scented bouquet
Miniature scented bouquets can be made from just a few scraps of scented foliage. Try combining spikes of lavender, small sprigs of herbs, rose blooms and buds, and fever-few flowers. These bouquets look pretty whether laid on a dressing table, propped on a shelf, or glued to baskets and boxes as decoration.

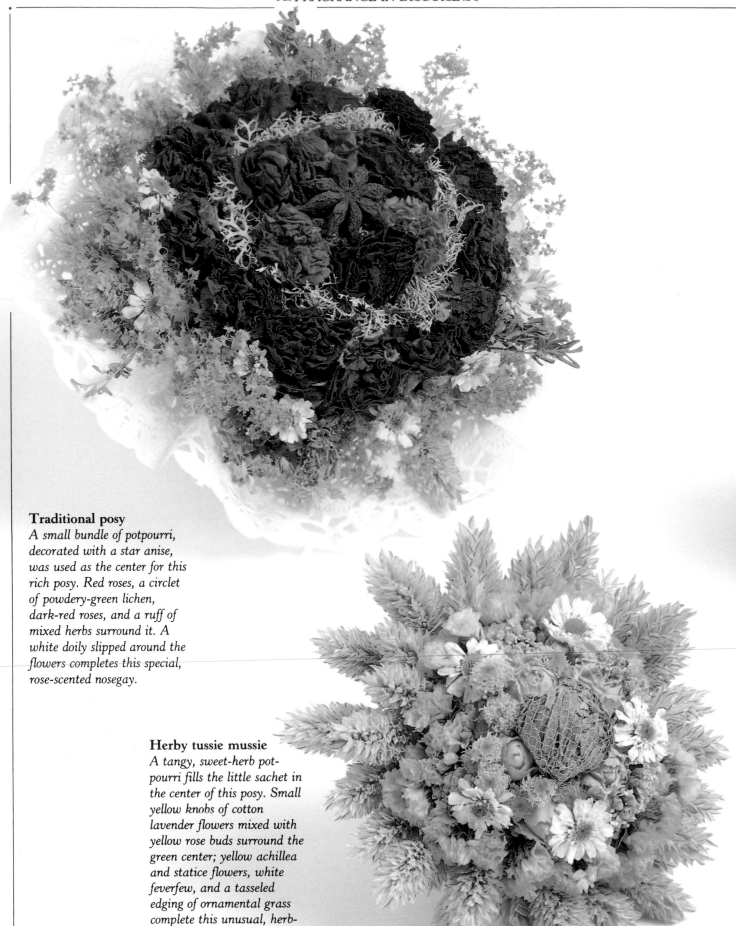

Traditional posy
A small bundle of potpourri, decorated with a star anise, was used as the center for this rich posy. Red roses, a circlet of powdery-green lichen, dark-red roses, and a ruff of mixed herbs surround it. A white doily slipped around the flowers completes this special, rose-scented nosegay.

Herby tussie mussie
A tangy, sweet-herb pot-pourri fills the little sachet in the center of this posy. Small yellow knobs of cotton lavender flowers mixed with yellow rose buds surround the green center; yellow achillea and statice flowers, white feverfew, and a tasseled edging of ornamental grass complete this unusual, herb-scented tussie mussie.

Victorian tussie mussie
Many flowers have been included in this substantial posy. Different shades of pink and red roses, elder flowers, and meadowsweet garland the lavender bag in the center. A mass of tiny white anaphalis flowers encircles the traditional arrangement.

Lavender-scented posy
The slate-blue center of this pastel-colored tussie mussie is surrounded by amethyst statice, pink rose buds, and heads of pale-green grass. White sneezewort flowers and red roses make up the outer garland, and a pale-mauve paper doily frames the posy.

Old-fashioned posy
In this charming little nosegay of pink and blue flowers, a lacy frill of pink, and the more unusual white, bistort frames a posy of larkspur flowers and

sweetly scented pink rose buds. The lavender center is in keeping with the pretty flowers used in this dusky-colored posy, to which a light-blue ribbon could be added.

Large country basket
This lovely basket, woven from leafy vine stems, offers an intriguing display of dried flowers and aromatic materials. Wired and decorated star anise, cinnamon sticks, and vanilla beans combine charmingly with a jumble of dried garden flowers. Scented bundles of rose-petal and lavender potpourri add to the sweet aroma.

Yellow and orange basket
The arrangement in this small, round basket is biased towards woods, berries, and fruit. Dried berries, fir cones, pine foliage, citrus peel, and a few sprigs of acid-yellow statice were mixed with star anise, cinnamon sticks, bundles of herb and lavender potpourri, a few fresh kumquats, and some unusual brown daisy flowers. A few drops of pine oil on the center of the cones blend with the fresh woodland scent of this rustic display.

Decorated basket
For added charm, the side of this humble basket (above) was decorated with pressed flowers, moss, and lichen. The arrangement is crammed with roses, elder blossoms, meadow-sweet, queen-anne's lace, lavender spikes, and other modest flowers. Little bundles of mixed potpourri, cinnamon sticks, star anise, and vanilla beans enhance the fragrance.

Balmy baths

Potpourri can be displayed in the bathroom, where it will scent the air with lavender, roses, pine, or sandalwood; or it can be used to perfume the bath water and soap.

The bathroom can be deliciously perfumed with potpourri displayed in bowls, jars, and even little scented baskets. Tuck pretty guest soaps among the scented flowers and leaves, so that they absorb the fragrance of the potpourri. Alternatively, make scented soap by melting unperfumed soap in a little floral water, adding a few drops of your favorite essential oil, and then leaving the mixture to set in an appropriate mold. Potpourris ideal for the bathroom range from pretty floral mixes to spiced and musky wood mixes, depending upon personal choice. Aromatic bath sachets are easy to make and delightful to use. Most fragrant flowers and sweet herbs are suitable for such mixes, and it is best to experiment to discover which combinations appeal to you the most. I have suggested one of my favorite recipes on page 84. Mix all the fragrant ingredients together and spoon the mixture into little muslin bags, or fill a jar with the potpourri and transfer some to a bag before each bath.

Potpourri baskets
Little hand-made Indian baskets, or khas dibbis, *make delightful containers for potpourri and soap, whether lemon-scented and homey or rose-scented and opulent.*

Dish of soaps
The traditional rose fragrance of the potpourri in this hyacinth-blue, scalloped china dish will fill the air in the bathroom in no time and impregnate the little pink and blue guest soaps.

Soap jar
This green-tinted glass storage jar makes an unusual translucent container for a sweet-smelling, mixed-flower potpourri and little cream hearts of soap.

❦ ROSE AND LAVENDER BAGS ❧

1oz strongly perfumed rose petals
1oz rose geranium leaves
1oz lavender
grated and dried rind of half a lemon
½oz rolled oats – optional (to soften the skin and give
volume to the ingredients)
*The quantities given here will fill about six small, well-packed
sachets and provide the bath water with a luxuriant perfume.*

Bath sachets
*There is nothing more
soothing and delightful than
relaxing in a bath that is
perfumed with flowers and
herbs from the garden. Roses
and lavender, chamomile,
rosemary, and basil, or
perhaps a tangy mix of balm
and lemon peel all make
lovely bath sachets. Bay,
mint, thyme, and scented-
geranium leaves can also be
used. The jars shown here
are decorated with pressed
queen-anne's lace; those on
the corks were sealed with
fragrant wax.*

CHAPTER THREE

Drying & Blending

A scented garden gives its owner much pleasure and a greater understanding of the plants whose flowers, leaves, roots, and even seeds can be used in the making of potpourri. Anyone can grow interesting fragrant plants no matter how small their garden. Gather blooms for potpourri when they are at their peak and scented foliage when it is at its lushest.

Flat blooms and individual leaves and petals lend themselves to drying flat, as do umbelliferous flowers, lichens, mosses, and berries. Many herbs and sprays of smaller flowers are traditionally dried by hanging them in bunches. Roses, too, can be dried by this method, but the loveliest open blooms should be dried flat and used to decorate the top of a mix. Potpourri can be made using either the dry or the moist method. Dry potpourris are easy to make, and look pretty, lending themselves to decorative presentation. Moist potpourris take longer to make, and are visually less attractive, but they are well worth the effort for their rich, long-lasting fragrances.

The fragrant garden

*Although we may not be able to re-create the fragrant
walled gardens of Ancient Persia in every detail, everyone can grow
scented plants and flowers, no matter how limited the space.*

Plants and flowers have many different perfumes. No garden is complete without perfume, whether light and floral, warm and spicy, cool and lemony, aromatic and herby, woody and earthy, or exotic and sensual. Perfume is at its strongest on a hot summer's day, but it *can* still hang in the air on a cold winter's day, and even immediately after heavy rain. Dry, windy conditions disperse the fragrance in a garden very quickly, and most flowers exude less scent in such a desiccating atmosphere.

The perfume of fragrant plants is dispatched in many different ways. Sometimes it is borne on the breeze: this is true of the scent of violets, musk roses, and sweetbriers. Many highly perfumed flowers, including a large number of roses, and some lilies, primroses, and lilacs, guard their perfume jealously, so that you are forced to bury your nose among their petals to discover their scent. Other plants, such as thymes, balms, and mints, must have their leaves crushed before they release their perfume. Flowers such as sweet rocket, summer jasmine, night-scented stocks, white *Nicotiana affinis*, and evening primrose only release their perfume in the evening or at night. Plants that contain coumarin are possibly one of the most fascinating groups of all. They release their aromatic scents only after they have been gathered and dried; woodruff and melilot belong to this group.

Although you will be able to grow countless varieties of scented plants together, you will find that you cannot grow every single fragrant plant in one garden no matter how extensive, as they can vary considerably in their growing requirements. For example, while many aromatic plants enjoy sunny, dry

conditions there are a few, such as primulas, mints, and woodruff, that prefer shady, damp situations. Obviously the two groups will not grow happily together. It *is* worth experimenting, though, for although a sun-loving Mediterranean plant will never grow in damp, shady conditions, a shade-loving plant may grow in full sun as long as you do not expect it to grow vigorously.

Fragrant plants are often quiet and unassuming in character. Flamboyant hybrids, with few exceptions, have little or no perfume, so the fragrant garden will contain a multitude of species plants, many of them old and humble in appearance. However, a dingy-looking plant can never be regarded as dull when one is aware of its scented flowers, foliage, or roots. For those not familiar with the scented garden, there will be all sorts of new delights: the discovery of hitherto unnoticed scented roots and seeds; balsamic scents, contained in flowers, buds, and stems; and the beautiful but ephemeral perfume of some flowers.

Many of the spring flowers are sweetly scented, and they are so delicate and appealing that I grow as many as I can. They include double and single primroses (not all are scented), white and purple violets, poached-egg flowers, scented daffodils and narcissi (early flowering 'Soleil d'Or' is a must), spicy wallflowers, hyacinths, lilies-of-the-valley, lilacs, azaleas, climbing vanilla-scented purple akebias, *Magnolia stellata*, *Viburnum burkwoodii*, and yellow buffaloberry. I grow and encourage wild flowers in my garden, too, including bluebells, chervil, woodruff, and pussy willow, the catkins of which, although not scented, look very pretty in so many potpourris.

Alchemilla mollis, astilbe, and fragrant-leaved Geranium procurrens *(above) grow at the edge of the courtyard. In the background grows* Cryptomeria japonica, *whose foliage is delightfully aromatic. In the flower borders surrounding the pond (right), gunnera, astrantia, balm, crocosmia, meadowsweet, and primulas grow.*

An abundance of scented flowers bloom during the summer months. Most important of all are the roses as they are all lovely when dried and used in a potpourri, particularly if they are scented, too. First and foremost comes *Rosa damascena* or the damask rose – I recommend the varieties 'Omar Khayam', 'Celsiana', and versicolor. Of the *Rosa alba* varieties, I recommend 'Maiden's Blush' and 'Celestial'. My favorite *Rosa gallica* or provins rose varieties include 'Cardinal de Richelieu', 'Tuscany', and *Rosa mundi*. Of the *Rosa centifolia* or cabbage rose varieties, I strongly recommend 'Fantin-Latour', 'Tour de Malakoff', 'Gloire de Malmaison', 'Blanche Moureau', and dear old 'William Lobb', the arched stems of which will always grab you as you walk past!

A plethora of fragrances

Other scented plants that flower in summer are the easily grown herbs such as thyme, lavender, mints, balms, sweet cicely, marsh-mallow, and marjoram; garden flowers include old pinks and carnations, lilies, *Primula sikkimensis*, buddleia, some hostas, phlox, and Solomon's seal. Summer-flowering climbers ideal for training up a wall of the house include jasmine, honeysuckle, clematis, *Rosa* 'Zéphirine Drouhin', and lovely violet-scented and violet-colored *Rosa* 'Veilchenblau' (my favorite rose). Many evening- and night-flowering blossoms, such as evening primrose, sweet rocket, some stocks, and *Nicotiana affinis*, disperse their fragrance so liberally that they will perfume an entire room if the window is left open.

Autumn also features many perfumed flowers and leaves, including costmary, myrtle, and elecampane. Some late-flowering day lilies are also perfumed, as are chrysanthemums (their leaves are also spicy and balsamic), and sweet olive. Perfumed flowers may also be found in some gardens during the winter months: their scent is always a pleasant surprise, as it is persistent and very sweet. The leaves of *Helleborus corsicus* are subtly musk-scented, and prettily veined, too, but the most alluringly perfumed flowers of the winter garden are wintersweet, *Lonicera fragrantissima*, *Viburnum* x *bodnantense*, and *Daphne odora*.

Many evergreens can be grown in the scented garden. Conifers offer a vast choice and are all pleasantly aromatic. Myrtle, bay, and eucalyptus grow happily in my garden, and I love to pinch their aromatic leaves when wandering around the garden during the cold winter months.

Mentha longifolia (*gray horse mint*) *grows in a lush, damp bed of* Polygonum campanulatum, *astilbe, giant grasses, double buttercup, white rosebay, willow herb, and a scented-leaf conifer.*

A few annuals and biennials have already been suggested, but there are one or two more that should be grown in the scented garden. Marigolds, in their bright orange, yellow, and apricot tones, brighten any sunny border. Mignonette is one of the most delightfully fragrant of flowers and will grow in any well-limed soil. Blue and mauve sweet peas, whose scent is the sweetest, can be grown in traditional ranks at the back of a border. Bedding verbena (*Verbena* x *hybrida*), and hawthorn-smelling cherry pie (*Heliotropium peruvianum*) are old-fashioned, sweetly perfumed plants that are easy and rewarding to grow.

Scented flowers for special places

For the water garden, sweet flag has pungent aromatic leaves and roots with fixative properties; the water hawthorn smells surprisingly sweet and spicy; and many water lilies are fragrant as well as being beautiful to look at in the middle of an overgrown garden pond.

Many herbs and aromatic plants can be grown in containers and window boxes. Lavender, thyme, mints, balms, and marjoram will thrive in tubs and containers, while lilies and sweet peas look good planted in pots. All these scented plants, and more, would perfume a balcony or terrace, and provide ingredients for potpourri.

One group of plants that will undoubtedly give much pleasure and can easily be grown indoors on a windowsill is the scented-leaf pelargoniums (or geraniums). Their leaves are finely cut and deliciously perfumed; their flowers are quite insignificant but the varying fragrance of their leaves is astounding. The ferny foliage can smell of apple, lemon, orange, nutmeg, peppermint, attar of roses, balsam, or pine. Their wonderful aroma is long lasting, and makes an excellent ingredient for a potpourri. You should therefore grow as many as you have room for.

Harvesting fragrant flowers

Aromatic plant material must be quite dry when gathered. Flowers must be in their prime or in bud, and foliage at its lushest. Do not gather damaged flowers or foliage, for they will never look good when dried. Most of the herbs and many of the flowers can be hang-dried (see p. 90). Individual leaves and blossoms are best dried flat (see p. 93), along with rose petals, and any flower heads that are being dried for decoration. All roots should be dried flat, after they have been thoroughly washed.

The trunk of this sycamore tree (above right) is encrusted with lichens, and, in the top right-hand and lower left-hand corners of the photograph, you can see the faintly violet-smelling lichen, oakmoss.

Acorus calamus, or sweet flag (right), grows among the parrot weed, water forget-me-nots, and white king cups in an overgrown pond. Both the roots and leaves of the sweet flag can be used.

Hang-drying

Hang-drying in bunches is the best way to dry herbs, such as lavender; flower sprays, such as lady's mantle; single flowers with larger heads, such as pinks; and large leaves, such as angelica.

Gather the herbs for drying just before they flower, unless of course you wish to dry the flowers as well. Pick flowers in bud or newly opened: a full-blown flower will never dry well. Make sure that the plant material is absolutely dry when you harvest it: noon on a fine day is ideal.

Any dry, airy place is suitable for hang-drying bunches of plant material: in a warm kitchen; over a radiator; in an airing cupboard; or even in an attic. String bunches of herbs and flowers where they can be seen for a continually changing decoration that allows you to observe the intriguing drying process. Attach a line or two across a room or cupboard and hang the bunches from them: you will be surprised at the number of bunches you can fit on a line only 2 feet long. Tie each bunch together and to the line with a band of nylon cut from a pair of tights: as each bunch dries and the stalks shrink, the nylon contracts, keeping the bunch tightly packed.

It is a good idea to remove most of the leaves from the flower stalks to allow the air to circulate freely around the stems and flower heads. This reduces the risk of mildew appearing before the plant material dries, and speeds up the drying process. If hang-drying roses, remove the thorns from the stalks for ease of handling. Bunch together no more than six sprays of herbs or flowers, to enable the material to dry out quickly and minimize the risk of mildew. Take great care when hang-drying flowers, particularly those with larger heads, which are easily crumpled during the drying process. Cut the stalks to different lengths so that, when bunched, the flower heads are staggered and do not touch one another. If sprays and umbels are too crowded, remove a flower head or two, but remember that the material shrinks as it dries, gradually requiring less room.

Herbs and flowers vary in the length of time that they take to become crisply dry, depending on how dry and airy the situation, and how thick the leaves and flowers. Do not hang them in strong sunlight, as, in most cases, the flower colors will fade, and remember that the faster the material dries, the more color it retains.

If you wish to store herbs and flowers after drying them, strip the sprays and stalks of leaves and flowers, and store them in a dry place. Keep them in boxes or large bags and label each of them for future reference.

DRYING A BUNCH OF FLOWERS

1 Choose a fine, dry day to pick the flowers. Select blooms that are in bud or newly opened, and do not pick too many, for they will wilt before you can deal with them. Sort through the fresh flowers carefully and discard any damaged ones.

2 Remove leaves from the flower stalks to allow air to circulate around them. If the leaves are aromatic or pretty, leave a few on the stems and remove and use them after the flowers have dried. Trim the stems to varying lengths.

3 Bunch together about six stems, making sure that the flower heads are not touching one another. Check that none of the petals is twisted or crushed. It is important to keep the heads separate, so that they dry quickly and remain intact.

4 Tie the bunch together with a band of elasticated nylon cut from a pair of tights. Loop the nylon around the stems and pull tight. Hang the bunch from a line strung across the drying area. Make sure that the flowers are not touching anything.

Subdued decoration

Making an attractive display in themselves, the bunches of herbs and flowers hang-drying here are (from left to right): variegated balm, lady's mantle, wormwood, and the enormous leaves of elecampane.

DRYING A BUNCH OF ROSES

Colorful display

Stagger the flower heads along the line to keep them well separated, otherwise they will dry crumpled and twisted. The bunches drying here are (from left to right): marsh-mallow, larkspur, bachelor's buttons, and modern and old-fashioned roses.

1 *When drying roses by the hanging method, it is best to remove all the thorns from the stems to make them easier and safer to handle. Cut them off with a sharp pair of scissors or snap them off.*

2 *To allow the air to circulate freely around the stalks and speed up the drying time, remove the leaves. Stagger the blooms in the bunch (see p. 90) and hang them to dry. (To dry leaves, see p. 93.)*

Drying flat

*If the material for drying is delicate or thick, if you need to use
only flower petals, or if you require decorative flower heads, then
it is best to dry the material flat.*

Fragile or dense flowers and leaves that are important scented ingredients in potpourri are best dried flat. They include fragrant jonquils, daffodils, irises, violets, lilies, honeysuckle, wallflowers, and some scented leaves, such as myrtle, eucalyptus, scented geranium, and sweetbrier.

In addition, I take great care to dry some flowers flat that are not necessarily perfumed, but whose shape and form are highly decorative. Nearly all the single flower heads that are to be used decoratively, such as cinquefoils, anemones, and roses, are better dried separately on a flat surface. Some decorative double flowers are also best dried flat. They include: double primroses, marsh marigolds, ranunculus, geums, feverfew, and double roses. Arrange such flowers carefully so that they dry in as natural a shape as possible. Another important group of flowers that I like to dry flat are the delicate umbelliferous blooms, which add a gossamer touch to a potpourri. They include the beautiful heads of queen-anne's lace, sweet cicely, chervil, and fennel flowers.

Rose petals, the most important ingredient in the majority of potpourris, can be dried only by the flat method. Gather them when they are quite dry – midday on a fine day is best – and choose petals from newly opened roses when their perfume is at its strongest. Dry the petals in layers no more than two petals deep and shuffle them daily. If the petals are to be used in a dry potpourri (see p. 96), leave them until they are crisply dry, usually about a week later. If the petals are to be used in a moist potpourri (see p. 98), they will be ready in a couple of days when placed in a warm, airy spot; they will then be partially dry and quite leathery.

Certain leaves, by virtue of their shape or color, should be carefully dried

flat for decorative purposes. They include the intriguingly fluted leaves of curled wood sage and forest-green *Rosa rugosa* leaves. Obviously, berries, fruits, and all citrus peels must be dried flat rather than by hanging.

To dry material flat, lay the petals, leaves, or fruit in a warm room on trays, sheets of recycled paper or newspaper, lengths of muslin stretched across two pieces of wood, or even specially built racks of narrow, closely slotted wood. Most flowers and leaves dry best when positioned face-up. Take care when laying them out: decorative blooms, such as double flower heads, should not, on any account, touch one another; and single petals will not dry out well if stacked more than two layers deep. The length of time needed for the material to dry ranges from a couple of days to a week or more, depending upon the drying conditions and the plant material. When ready, it should feel crisp and warm to the touch, and the colors should remain bright, particularly if the plant material has been kept out of strong sunlight. In fact, most dark-red roses will retain their color even if dried in the sun. The material will, of course, shrink considerably during the drying process. If you do not wish to use the material right away, store it in individually marked boxes in a warm, dry place, such as an airing cupboard.

The many-splendored rose
Most parts of the rose plant can be used in a potpourri. If it is to be highly perfumed, the petals will play the most important role. Whole blooms of the perfumed rose will enrich a mix visually, as will opening buds, and even small, tight, green ones. Many rose leaves dry to a luxuriant green, and some are slightly perfumed, as are a number of rose roots.

Rose blooms for decoration

Rose leaves

Rose petals

Fuchsias

The drooping blooms of fuchsias (below) have been likened to dancers, and they do appear to have wonderfully frilled petticoats. There are many varieties that can be grown, from the very pale pink F. magellanica, to great, vivid hybrids. For such succulent flowers, they dry surprisingly well, and can make the top of a potpourri resemble a lavish Mexican embroidery.

Daucus carota var. carota
Queen-anne's lace

Fuchsia magellanica
Fuchsias

Queen-anne's lace

The lacy, umbelliferous flowers of queen-anne's lace (above) have no perfume but are essential for creating a gossamer look in a floral potpourri. They also look very attractive when added to a green herb potpourri. I also frequently use the exquisite pale almond-green flowers of the edible carrot.

Berries and small fruits

Eye-catching and colorful berries (below) make striking additions to a potpourri. Rose hips vary considerably in shape and color, from the elliptical hips of Rosa moyesii through the fat, rusty ones of R. rugosa to the black R. pimpinellifolia hips. While rowan berries remain brightly colored when dried, hawthorn and cotoneaster berries deepen in color. Crab apples make fascinating little, shriveled fruits when dried.

Rosa pimpinellifolia
Rose hips

Sorbus aucuparia
Mountain ash hips

Malus floribunda
Crab apples

Rosa moyesii
Rose hips

Malus purpurea
Crab apple

Rosa rugosa
Rose hip

Anemone
coronaria 'De Caen'
'De Caen' anemones

Anemones

Ideal for drying flat, anemones (right) are charming when used decoratively. Try drying the lovely white or pink velvety blooms of the Japanese anemone, or the rich, black-centered blooms of the 'De Caen' varieties — second to none for sheer impact. Of the more substantial varieties, the brilliant red and blue anemones mix well with brown woods and fir cones, and the oranges, yellows, and greens of citrus fruits; while the fragile pastel-colored ones are better suited to country mixes.

Anemone x hybrida
Anemones

Teucrium scorodonia
'Crispum Marginatum'
Curled wood sage

Bergamot
Grown in our gardens for
centuries, the old purple
bergamot (right) is still a
favorite. All varieties of
bergamot have delicious,
orange-scented leaves. The
flowers are also fragrant, and
their unusual shape makes
them perfect for decorating the
surface of a potpourri.

Monarda media
Bergamot

Curled wood sage
The deep pine-green leaves of
curled wood sage (above) retain
their color well, and their
elaborately ruffled edges are
sensational. They are ideal for
making decorative borders in
an open potpourri. The plant's
near relative – the wild wood
sage – has dark, velvety leaves,
which are also worth drying.

Potentilla spp.
Shrubby and herbaceous
cinquefoils

Cinquefoils
Cinquefoils (left) are easy to
grow, and add an enormous
variety of color to a potpourri.
Scatter the yellow and orange
blooms in the nooks and
crannies of a bulky citrus
potpourri; garnish an
Elizabethan potpourri with the
rich red ones; and use the
black-centered, strawberry-pink
flowers to enliven any kind
of potpourri.

Tree mallow
Tree mallow flowers (below),
which are pink when fresh, dry
to resemble scraps of blue tissue
paper. Flowers from this family
are exciting to dry, as one is
never certain exactly what
shade of blue they will turn out
to be. With any luck, it will be
a very intense parma-violet,
which is bound to dominate a
potpourri.

Lavatera arborea
Tree mallow

Hydrangeas
The lovely misty colors of blue,
pink, and cream hydrangea
flowers (right), and the sheer
volume of their blooms, make
them indispensable to
potpourri. Perhaps the loveliest
of all potpourris is one in which
hydrangeas of all the sugared-
almond colors are mixed with
herbs and some dark green
leaves. You can even spray
hydrangea flowers gold or silver
to decorate such a potpourri,
which is the prettiest of mixes.

Hydrangea spp.
Hydrangeas

Making potpourri

*There are two basic methods of making potpourri: the dry
method and the moist method. Dry potpourris are more
attractive to look at but moist potpourris are more highly scented.*

There are five basic groups of ingredients in a dry pot-pourri: scented flowers, herbs, spices, fixatives, and essential oils. The first and most important group is that of the scented and decorative materials, which may be flowers, wood, bark, or fruit (see pp. 100–122). These will set the theme of your potpourri. Secondly come the scented herbs (see p. 102), of which lavender is the most important and most frequently used. Rosemary, mints, balms, bergamot, and thymes are also commonly used. Their perfumes add interest to the dominant perfume of a mix, providing it with more complexity.

The next group is the spices (see p. 112) with their warm, sweet smell: they add richness, depth, and sometimes a piquant note to the general bouquet. The fourth group is composed of fixatives (see p. 120), without which the per-fume of the potpourri would very quickly be lost. They fix, or hold, and absorb the scents of all the other ingredients, often contributing their own fragrance as well. There are fixatives in all groups of vegetative materials, but you can rely on the easily obtainable orris root powder and gum benzoin, unless, of course, you have other, more obscure fixatives on hand in the kitchen.

The last group comprises the essential oils (see p. 122), which can either dictate the perfume of a potpourri entirely, or simply contribute to it, depending on how much scented plant material you have included. Dried citrus peel (see p. 118) can also be added to a potpourri.

The two methods

A dry potpourri is by far the easiest to make and the most popular, for the potpourri is finished as soon as the dried materials have been mixed, although the mix should be allowed to mature for a few weeks before being displayed in a room or used to fill pillows or sachets.

Moist potpourri is more time-consuming to create. It is made in two stages: creating a moist "stock-pot" of highly scented petals, which involves a curing process, and then combining this mixture with all the other dry ingredients. The cured stock-pot replaces the first group of ingredients in a dry potpourri. The perfume of a moist potpourri is delicious. Not only is it stronger than that of a dry mix, but it is alluringly rich, too. Moist potpourris are not pretty to look at, so they are best contained in a jar or box with a perforated lid to allow the scent to escape.

MAKING A DRY POTPOURRI

*1 In a small bowl, place the ground spices
(2 teaspoons cinnamon powder and
½ teaspoon grated nutmeg) and the fixative
(1oz orris root powder). Add six drops of
essential oil. If you want a very strongly
scented mix, add a little more oil.*

*2 Thoroughly mix the oil, fixative, and
spices. Rub the mixture between your
first two fingers and thumb as though you
were rubbing fat into flour. This will ensure
that all the scent of the essential oil is fixed
and provide a strong bouquet.*

*3 In a separate mixing bowl, place the
remaining dry ingredients (1 quart
fragrant petals, 2oz mixed sweet herbs, 1oz
lavender, ½ teaspoon whole cloves, and ¼
vanilla bean). In a dry place, store the
decorative dried flower heads.*

Essential oil

Mixing bowl

Small bowl

Spices and fixative

Flower petals

Airtight container

Mixed sweet herbs, including lavender

4 Pour the mixture of fixative, spices, and oil into the mixing bowl that contains the bulk of the dry ingredients. Mix together thoroughly to ensure that the oil, fixative, and spices are evenly distributed throughout the potpourri.

5 Place the mixture in an airtight container and leave in a dark place for at least six weeks. Shake the container every day for the first week. The longer you leave the potpourri, the more mature the fragrance will become.

6 After a minimum of six weeks, transfer the potpourri to a decorative open bowl. Decorate the top with the dried flower heads that you set aside. Reseal in the storage container any of the mix you do not yet wish to use.

MAKING A MOIST POTPOURRI

1 To make the stock-pot, place a half-inch layer of partially dried rose petals in a storage container. Sprinkle over the top some coarse salt (a third of the thickness of the petals). Add a second layer of petals and press down firmly with your hand. Spoon on top another layer of salt.

2 Sprinkle a pinch of brown sugar and a few drops of brandy on this and every subsequent second layer of petals and salt. Continue layering with petals, salt, sugar, and brandy until the container is full. Seal and leave to cure for two months. Check and drain if necessary.

3 Crumble the cured cake of rose petals or stock-pot into a bowl containing the spices, herbs, fixatives, and essential oils required by the recipe. Mix thoroughly and allow to cure for a further three weeks. Transfer to a bowl and decorate or to a lidded, perforated potpourri dish.

Rose petals

Salt

Sugar

Storage container

Spoon

Brandy

Mixing bowl

Stock-pot

CHAPTER FOUR
Perfume Portfolio

Rose blooms and petals are the most important ingredients in the majority of potpourris: damask, provins, and cabbage roses exude the strongest perfumes. Herbs of all kinds, from the gently scented, green-leaved ones to the aromatic gray-leaved herbs of the Mediterranean, all play their part in potpourri, as do the many scented garden flowers that retain their perfume when dried. Even brightly colored, unperfumed flowers can be used in potpourri to improve the color and texture of a mix, and roots and seeds add to the overall bouquet and appearance. The list of scented plants that can be grown is enormous: while some plants have only aromatic roots, or perhaps seeds, others are scented throughout, and some have a different perfume in each part of the plant.

Roses

Rose blooms and petals are the most important ingredients in many potpourris. They add a beautiful perfume and a wonderful depth of color. Of the rich, dark, old-fashioned roses, the damask and centifolia varieties emit the strongest scents, although all the old roses are fragrant and perfectly suited to potpourri. Many of the colorful modern hybrid tea roses also have a sweet fresh perfume, and their elegant, half-open buds accentuate the charm of a mix. Just as lovely are the large petals of many of the hybrid teas. The dark-red ones are my favorites, as their color and velvety texture lends rich substance to a potpourri.

Old-fashioned and shrub roses
These sumptuous roses contain distinctive perfumes, from the heavy scents of the damask and centifolia roses to the peppery fragrance of 'Cecily Brunner'.

Modern roses
The sophisticated beauty of these roses is entirely different from the unruly charm of the old-fashioned and shrub roses. From magenta to blush-pink and from apricot to primrose-yellow, the range of color of the hybrid teas is enormous and they dry very well.

Subtly scented herbs

The lovely flowers of this selection of gently perfumed herbs range from soft sprays of meadowsweet to imposing yellow heads of achillea, and the leaves vary greatly in shape, texture, and color. All are easy to obtain and grow, and every one can make a valuable contribution to a potpourri. Even flowers from the humble mint look delightful when dried, and the leaves of this herb are especially useful when creating a fresh, piquant potpourri, adding both strength of color and scent.

Thymus *x* citriodorus
Lemon thyme

Salvia pratensis tenorii
Meadow sage

Mentha *x* spicata
Spearmint

Apium
graveolens
Smallage

Mentha *x* piperita
Peppermint

Rosmarinus officinalis 'Aureus'
Variegated rosemary

Artemisia dracunculus
French tarragon

Salvia officinalis 'Purpurascens'
Purple sage

Ocimum basilicum
'Purpurascens'
Dark opal basil

Inula magnifica
Elecampane

Achillea millefolium
Wild yarrow

Achillea millefolium
'Cerise Queen'
Yarrow

Achillea filipendulina
Yarrow

Melissa officinalis *'Aurea'*
Lemon-scented variegated balm

Filipendula palmata
Meadowsweet

Filipendula ulmaria
Queen of the meadow

Filipendula rubra
Queen of the Prairie

Strongly scented herbs

Many of the herbs shown on these pages come from the Mediterranean region, and prefer a warm, dry situation in the garden. Soft to the touch, their lovely foliage (and occasionally their flowers) is usually aromatic. Lavender, with its distinctive fragrance, is a traditional and often essential ingredient in a potpourri, and can be included in almost any mix. The silver leaves and the often pale-colored flowers add refinement.

Salvia officinalis *'Tricolor'*
Variegated sage

Lavandula angustifolia
Lavender

white

Salvia sclarea
Clary sage

mauve

pink

Lavandula stoechas
French lavender

Origanum dictamnus
Cretan dittany

Pelargonium crispum *'Variegatum'*
Scented white variegated geranium

Artemisia ludoviciana *'Silver Queen'*
White sage

Althaea officinalis
Marsh-mallow

Mentha longifolia
Horsemint

Perovskia atriplicifolia
Russian sage

Verbena hastata
Blue vervain

Artemisia pedemontana
Artemisia

Garden flowers

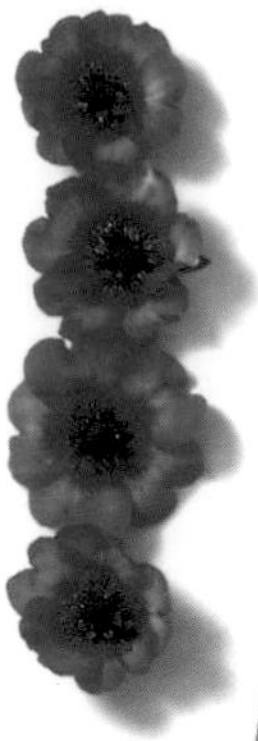

The flowers shown on this and the following three pages are pretty, prolific, and easy to grow. They are not all scented, but they all enhance the look of a potpourri. Pink, purple, and blue flowers always look lovely combined, while yellow and orange blooms mingled with green herbs make the brightest of mixes. Larkspurs retain their color well, particularly the blue varieties, while the dainty, lime-green flowers of lady's mantle will lighten any mix. I grow queen-anne's lace as a garden flower, using the exquisite pale green or pink dried umbels that look like little lacy mats to decorate many mixes.

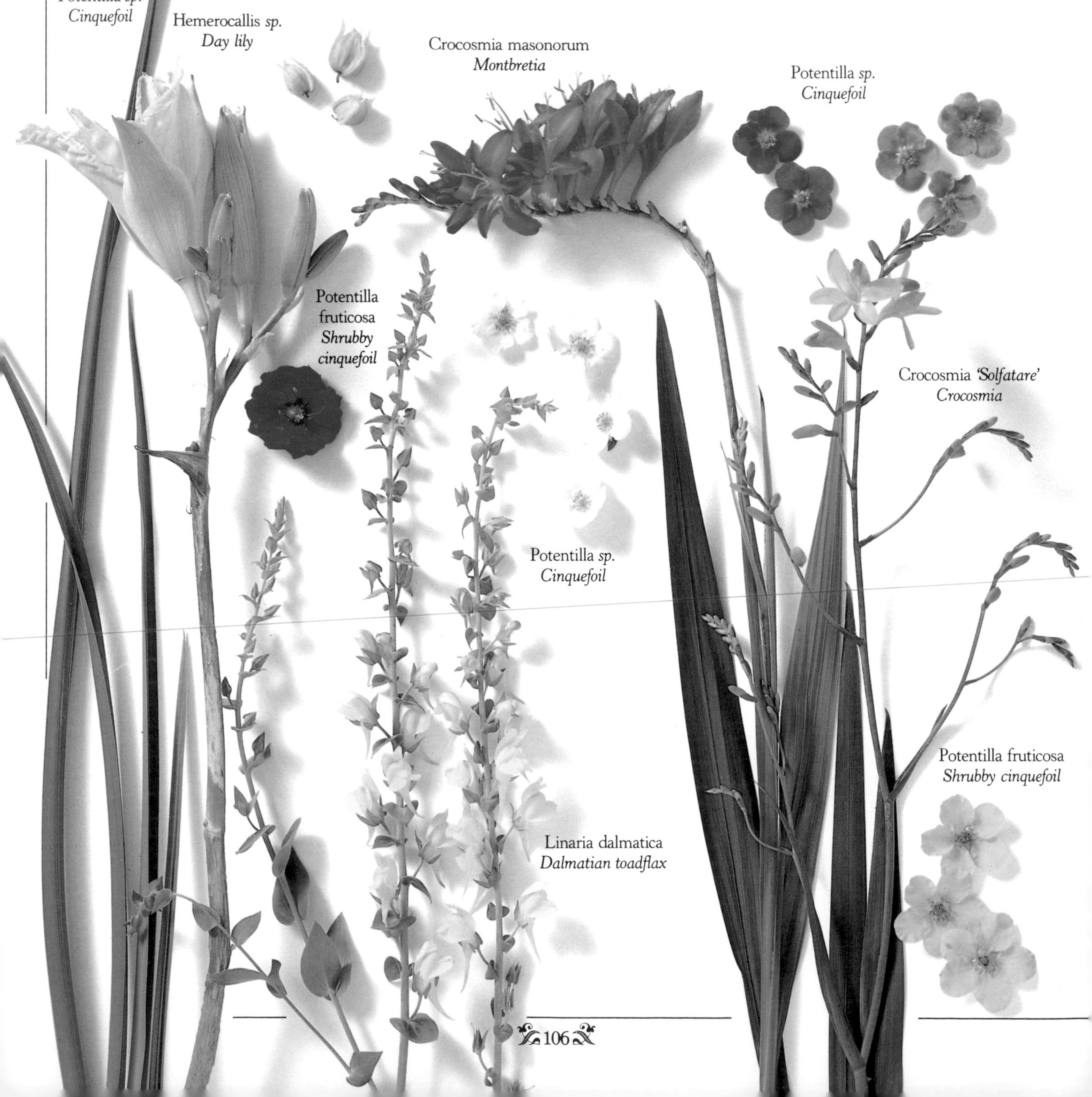

Potentilla *sp.*
Cinquefoil

Hemerocallis *sp.*
Day lily

Crocosmia masonorum
Montbretia

Potentilla *sp.*
Cinquefoil

Potentilla
fruticosa
*Shrubby
cinquefoil*

Crocosmia 'Solfatare'
Crocosmia

Potentilla *sp.*
Cinquefoil

Linaria dalmatica
Dalmatian toadflax

Potentilla fruticosa
Shrubby cinquefoil

Potentilla *sp.*
Cinquefoil

Lythrum virgatum
Loosestrife

Clematis viticella
Vine bower

Knautia
macedonica
Knautia

Cosmos atrosanguineus
Cosmos

Astilbe chinensis
Astilbe

Hydrangea *sp.*
Hydrangea

Daucus carota var. carota
Queen-anne's lace

Centauria cyanus
Bachelor's buttons

Nigella damascena
Love-in-a-mist

Astrantia maxima
Masterwort

Calendula officinalis
Pot marigold

Chrysanthemum maximun
Shasta daisy

Alchemilla mollis
Lady's mantle

Delphinium consolida
Larkspur

Achillea ptarmica
Sneezewort

Cosmos bipinnatus
Cosmos

Astrantia major
Masterwort

Dianthus *sp.*
Pinks

Polygonum
campanulatum
Knotweed

Nepeta
x faassenii
Catmint

Aromatic garden foliage

Many of the highly ornamental plants from which the foliage on these pages is taken, have lent interest and character to our gardens for centuries. Their aromatic leaves – whether tough, shiny, and evergreen, or soft, warm, and herbaceous – have also added color, texture, and fragrance to many potpourris. Pungent sweet flag, with its long, pointed leaves, also has aromatic roots, and both the leaves and the root can be used as fixatives (see p. 120) in potpourri. The cockled leaves of the curly-leaved wood sage dry to delicate little frilled mats that always make an attractive decoration for a mix displayed in an open bowl. Much conifer foliage is fragrant as well as highly textural, and both the tips and the berries of juniper are aromatic.

Phlomis fruticosa
Jerusalem sage

Pittosporum tobira
Pittosporum

Salvia splendens
Red salvia

Pelargonium
macrorrhizum
Scented-leaf geranium

Hypericum patulum
St. John's wort

Olearia
Daisy bush

Myrica gale
Sweet gale

Monarda
media
Bergamot

Matteuccia
struthiopteris
Ostrich fern

Acorus calamus
Sweet flag

Myrtus communis
Myrtle

Artemisia
abrotanum
Lad's love

Filipendula
hexapetala
Dropwort

Juniperus
communis
Juniper

Teucrium
corodonia
urly-leaved
wood sage

Picea smithiana
Orange-tipped spruce

Sanguisorba canadensis
Burnet

Spices, seeds, woods, conifers, & roots

Warm, sweet-smelling spices, aromatic woods, and softly scented roots are all important to potpourri, lending a depth and piquancy to the fragrance of a mix. Most recipes call for some spices, which range in aroma from subtle and shadowy to strong and dominant, and a few call for scented woods, such as conifer needles, buds, and tips. Sweet flag, geranium, sweet cicely, angelica, and elecampane all have aromatic roots as well as scented leaves. Decorative seed heads, such as fluffy clematis, pussy willow catkins, and tiny alder cones, all make a potpourri more interesting to look at, as do the delightful little scaled lockets of hop, which can also be used in sleep pillows.

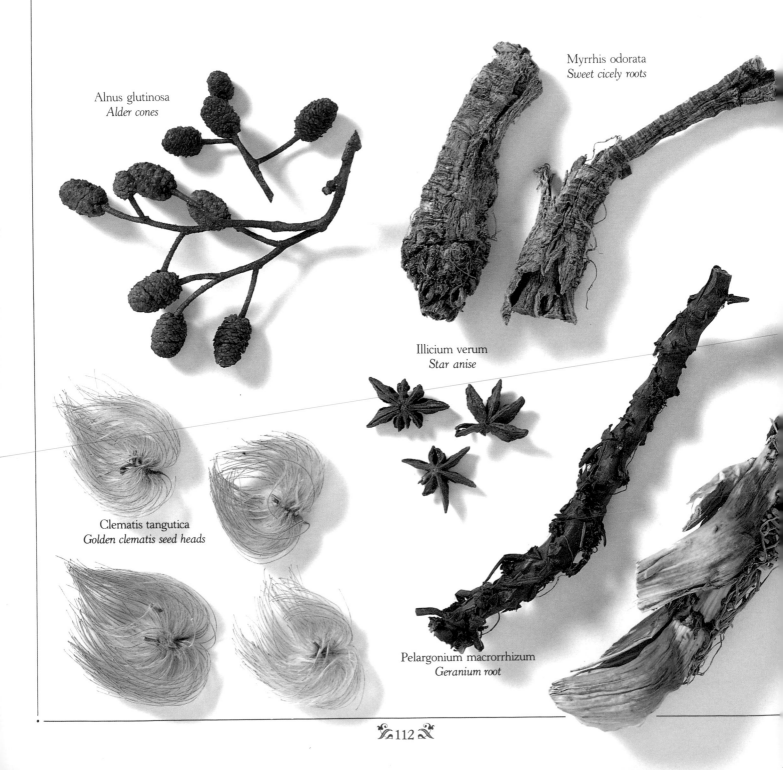

Alnus glutinosa
Alder cones

Myrrhis odorata
Sweet cicely roots

Illicium verum
Star anise

Clematis tangutica
Golden clematis seed heads

Pelargonium macrorrhizum
Geranium root

Geum urbanum
Herb bennet

Angelica archangelica
Angelica root

Acorus calamus
Sweet flag root

Inula magnifica
Elecampane root

Elettaria cardamomum
Cardamom seeds

Pinus *sp.*
Large pine cone

Pinus *sp.*
Small pine cones

Cinnamomum zeylanicum
Cinnamon bark

Logwood chips

Quassia armara
Quassia chips

Myristica fragrans
Mace

Cedrus *sp.*
Cedar wood shavings

Pimenta dioica
Allspice

Carum carvi
Caraway seeds

Populus candicans
Balsam poplar buds

Cedrus *sp.*
Cedar petals

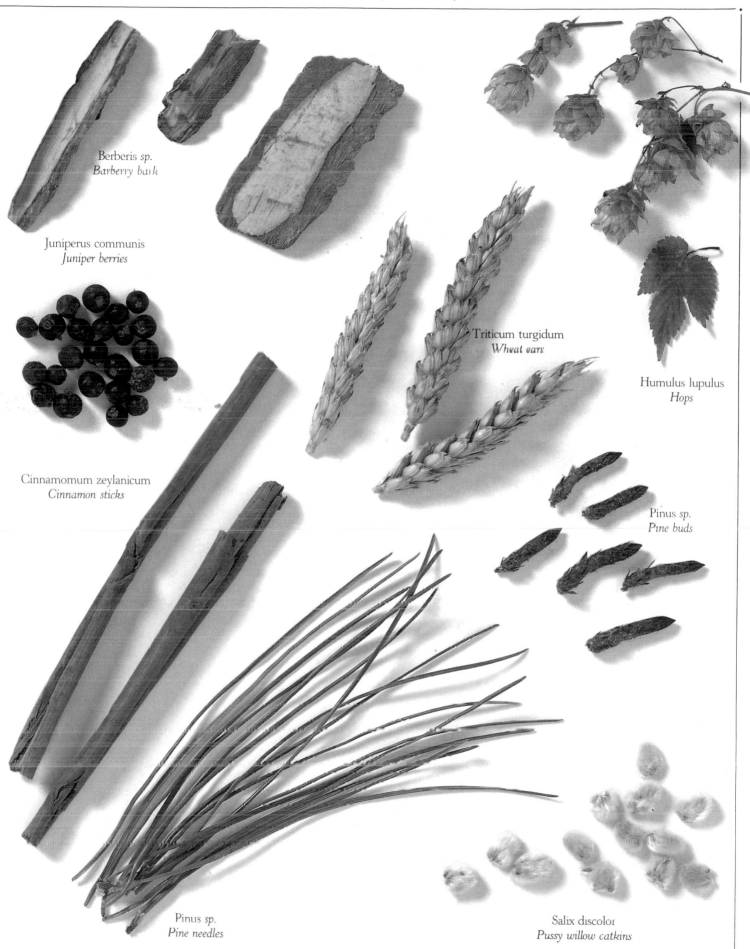

Berberis *sp.*
Barberry bark

Juniperus communis
Juniper berries

Cinnamomum zeylanicum
Cinnamon sticks

Triticum turgidum
Wheat ears

Humulus lupulus
Hops

Pinus *sp.*
Pine buds

Pinus *sp.*
Pine needles

Salix discolor
Pussy willow catkins

Berries & small fruits

Many of the autumnal berries make decorative additions to a potpourri. Large red *Rosa rugosa* hips, if dried slowly, become intriguing orange knobs as they shrivel. Both black burnet rose hips and sloe berries look distinctive in a mix, and *Rosa moyesii* hips are striking when dried, becoming wrinkled, leathery, pale orange torpedos. All sorts of crab apples can be dried, from plum-sized, purple ones to small, shiny, scarlet ones. Their appearance when dried is quite different from their look when fresh: their crinkly dried skins are fascinating and add to the jumble of textures in a potpourri. Mountain ash berries dry outstandingly well: their brilliant colors actually intensify during the process. Both the wild and cultivated hawthorn species have interesting fruits. The larger cotoneaster berries add to the reds of autumn: try to pick bunches that contain a few green berries as well as red, for the variety of color they add to a mix. Ensure that you are familiar with the poisonous berries (see p. 123) before you pick any.

Crataegus prunifolia
Hawthorn berries

Mixed dried berries

Prunus spinosa
Sloe berries

Rosa rugosa
Rose hips

Rosa moyesii
Rose hips

Sorbus aucuparia
European mountain ash hips

Cotoneaster franchetii
Cotoneaster berries

Crataegus x lavallei
Hawthorn berries

Rosa pimpinellifolia
Rose hips

Cotoneaster x watereri 'Cornubia'
Cotoneaster berries

Malus robusta
Crab apples

Malus floribunda
Showy crab apples

Citrus fruits

Dried citrus fruit peel has been used in potpourri for centuries. Oranges, lemons, and limes are the citrus fruits most commonly used in potpourri, but there are many others available, and it is worth experimenting with them to see which you like best. Instead of ordinary orange peel, try the tangy-scented clementine or tangerine peel to add quite a different note to a potpourri. For a potpourri with a stronger fragrance, try using the peel of Seville oranges, which have the most penetrating aroma of all oranges. Peel the fruit in long, thin strips, or in quartered portions, and dry flat in a warm oven. When dry, divide the thin strips into small pieces, or grind them, depending on the appearance you wish to create in the potpourri. Leave the quartered pieces as they are, as their chunky appearance adds textural interest to a mix.

The fresh, bright greens, oranges, yellows, and apricot colors of citrus fruits mingle attractively with flowers and woods, and retain their fragrance for a long time. They can also be used whole to make piquant pomanders (see p. 72) for hanging in cupboards and from ceiling beams. A bowl of orange, lemon, lime, and grapefruit pomanders looks and smells delicious.

Citrus x paradisi 'Ruby'
Ruby grapefruit peel

Fortunella japonica
Kumquats

Citrus x paradisi
Grapefruit peel

Citrus aurantium
Orange and orange peel

Citrus aurantiifolia
Lime and lime peel

Citrus limon
Lemon and lemon peel

Aromatic fixatives

Fixatives play a key role in potpourri: they absorb and retain the volatile scented oils that give the flowers, herbs, and other ingredients their perfume. If they were not used, a potpourri would quickly lose its beautiful fragrance. Most fixatives are aromatic in themselves and add to the bouquet of a potpourri as well as fixing its scent. A mix will usually call for at least two fixatives.

Fixative properties are found in certain gums, resins, roots, seeds, spices, herbs, woods, leaves, flowers, and even lichens. Orris root powder and gum benzoin are easiest to obtain and most commonly used, but cinnamon powder (or broken cinnamon sticks), cloves, and nutmeg are also effective fixatives and are usually on hand in the kitchen. Cumin and coriander can also be used but it is better to use the oil from these two fixatives. Sweet cicely seeds, angelica seeds, and chamomile flowers are all fixatives that can be grown in the garden, and the lovely gray lichen, known as oakmoss, which is an excellent and pretty fixative, can be found in England growing on trees, wooden fences, and gates. The soft, sweet odor of vanilla beans and tonka, or tonquin, beans will enhance the fragrance of a mix as well as hold its perfume. All the fixatives shown on these two pages are popular vegetable fixatives, which are easy to obtain. Others, which are not shown but which can easily be grown or obtained, include: the resins of myrrh, galbanum, and labdanum; roots of spikenard, sweet flag, elecampane, and geranium; musk seed; oil of sandalwood, cassia, cedarwood, cypress, patchouli, ilang-ilang, basil, marjoram, and thyme; and the leaves of sweet woodruff, melilot, myrtle, cistus, lemon verbena, and patchouli.

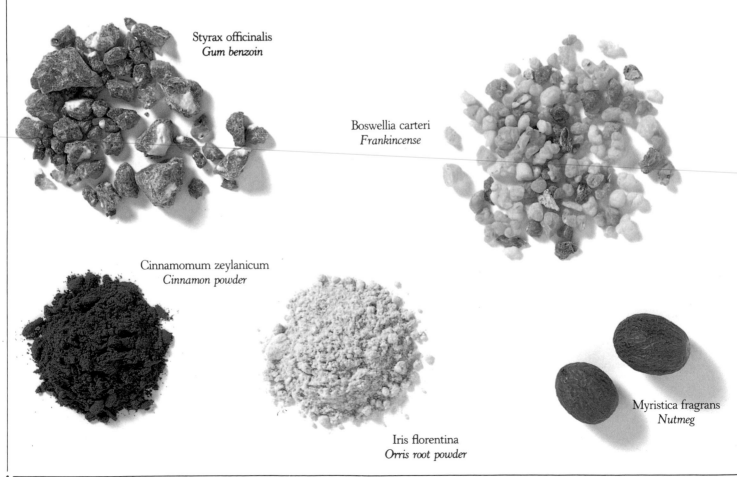

Styrax officinalis
Gum benzoin

Boswellia carteri
Frankincense

Cinnamomum zeylanicum
Cinnamon powder

Myristica fragrans
Nutmeg

Iris florentina
Orris root powder

Anthemis nobilis
Chamomile flowers

Evernia purpuracea
Oakmoss

Eugenia aromatica
Cloves

Myrrhis odorata
Sweet cicely seeds

Dipteryx odorata
Tonka beans

Cuminum cyminum
Cumin seeds

Angelica archangelica
Angelica seeds

Coriandrum sativum
Coriander

Vanilla planifolia
Vanilla bean

Essential oils

Extracted essential oils give potpourri its strongest perfume. Just a single oil or a combination of oils can be used, depending upon what is available or appropriate to the recipe.

Essential oils are found in perfumed flowers, leaves, roots, and even seeds. The buds of balsam poplar, birch, cassia, cloves; and the flowers of pink and carnation, heliotrope, honeysuckle, hyacinth, jasmine, jonquil, lilac, lily-of-the-valley, orange blossom, rose, sweet pea, violet, wallflower, and ilang-ilang all contain essential oils. They are also to be found in the leaves and stems of cinnamon, patchouli, garden geranium, and vervain; and in the barks of cassia, cedar, and cinnamon. The woods of cedar and sandal, and the roots or rhizomes of sweet flag, ginger, iris florentine, elecampane, geranium, angelica, sweet cicely, roseroot, and some eryngiums contain essential oils; as do citrus fruits, the seeds of cardamom, cumin, fennel, musk, angelica, sweet cicely, nutmeg, and star anise, and the resins of olibanum (frankincense), labdanum, myrrh, and storax.

The perfume of all these essential oils ranges from the highly citric, through the floral and spicy, to the strong and highly persistent aromas of wood, oakmoss, patchouli, iris, and even the delicious vanilla.

Liberating perfumes

On a hot summer's day the air in the garden may be filled with fragrance, for many flowers will release their perfume freely in the heat of the sun. Other perfumes are liberated when a plant is touched or bruised. Some leaves, roots, and seeds have to be crushed, however, to liberate (or discharge) the scent contained within them.

To obtain an essential oil for use in perfumery, it is necessary to separate it from the plant material by any one of the following three methods: expression, distillation, or extraction. In the first, pressure is applied to the plant material to squeeze out the oil: citrus fruit oils are obtained in this manner. In the distillation process, fragrant material is placed in boiling water, so that when the essential oil evaporates, it mixes with the steam from the water. Then, when the steam condenses, the oil separates from the water and floats on the surface.

Extracting essential oils

Extraction involves the infusion of the fragrant plant material in fat, oil, or spirit. There are two ways of extracting essential oils. In the first – *enfleurage* – the fragrant plant material is infused in cool olive oil. When the fragrant oils have been released into the olive oil, the exhausted flowers and petals are removed and replaced with fresh ones. Flowers and oil are most easily separated by straining the oil, pressing the flowers down firmly. This process is repeated until the oil is saturated with perfume. In the second method of extraction – maceration – the oil is heated to cause the perfumes to be more readily given up by the fragrant materials. The container of oil is placed in a pan of hot water for a few hours and the plant material changed daily until the oil is saturated with fragrance as before.

The essential oils that I use most frequently are the traditional rose and lavender oils, which are appropriate for so many recipes. However, experiment with different oils to discover the combinations of scented flowers and perfume you prefer. Try making some essential oils yourself by extracting them, using the *enfleurage* or maceration methods, which are both easy to do at home.

Lavender oil

Frankincense

Rose oil

Patchouli oil

Bergamot oil

Conservation of wildflowers

When looking out of doors for wild flowers and plants suitable for drying for potpourri, it is wise to take along an illustrated guide book for identification of the flora you encounter. In the United States, there are over a hundred rare species of plants and flowers that are protected by law – and several thousand more in line to be protected.

The laws differ from state to state but are particularly strong on Federal lands where penalties for removing plants can be heavy. Please be aware that a plant that is common in one region of the United States may be considered rare in another region and, therefore, protected by law.

To find out more about the wild plants and flowers that are protected in your area, you can consult reference books and directories at your local library, or contact a wildlife agency or regional office of the US Fish and Wildlife Service.

POISONOUS BERRIES

The fruits of the following woodland or garden plants are known to be poisonous to man and animals. Avoid using them in potpourri, no matter how attractive they might look. In addition to these specific plants, avoid picking any white fruits that you come across.

Common name	Scientific name	Common name	Scientific name
Black locust	Robinia pseudoacacia	Mayapple, mandrake	Podophyllum peltatum
Castor-bean	Ricinus communis	Poison ivy	Rhus radicans
Common moonseed	Menispermum canadense	Poison sumac	Rhus vernix
Deadly nightshade	Solanum dulcamara	Pokeweed	Phytolacca americana
English ivy	Hedera helix	Spindle tree	Euonymus europaea
February daphne	Daphne mezereum	Wisteria	Wisteria spp.
Golden-chain	Laburnum anagyroides	Yews	Taxus spp.

Suppliers

SUPPLIERS
Some have both a retail and a mail order business. Call for information.

MAIL ORDER SOURCES
for essences, fixatives, dried flowers and other potpourri ingredients

Tom Thumb Workshops
Route 13, P. O. Box 357
Mappsville, VA 23407
(804) 824-3507
Shop on premises

Cambridge Chemists, Inc.
21 East 65th Street
New York, NY 10021
(212) 734-5678

Caswell-Massey Catalog Division
111 8th Avenue
Suite 1532
New York, NY 10011
(212) 620-0900

Well-Sweep Herb Farm
317 Mount Bethel Road
Port Murray, NJ 07865
(201) 852-5390
Essential oils and fixatives

RETAIL SOURCES
for essences, fixatives, dried flowers, and other potpourri ingredients

Aphrodisia
282 Bleecker Street
New York, NY 10014
(212) 989-6440
Catalog available

Angelica's Traditional Herbs and
    Foods, Inc.
147 First Avenue
New York, NY 10003
(212) 529-4335

Gilbertie's Herb Gardens
Sylvan Lane
Westport, CT 06880
(203) 227-4175
Herbs and essential oils

Kiehl's
109 Third Avenue
New York, NY 10003
(212) 475-3698, 677-3171
Essential oils

Caswell-Massey
518 Lexington Avenue
New York, NY 10017
(212) 755-2254

Caswell-Massey Boston
Copley Place
100 Huntington Avenue
Boston, MA 02116
(617) 437-9292

Caswell-Massey
58 Phipps
3500 Peachtree Road N.E.
Atlanta, GA 30326
(404) 261-9415

Caswell-Massey of Washington D.C.
Pavilion at the Old Post Office
1100 Pennsylvania Avenue N.W.
Washington, DC 20004
(202) 898-1833

Caswell-Massey San Francisco
Stonestown Galleria
3251 20th Avenue
San Francisco, CA 94132
(415) 681-1606

Index

E

Egyptian perfumiers 6
elecampane 8, *103, 113,* 120
Elettaria cardamomum 113
Elizabethan potpourri 45
enfleurage 122
equipment 56–7, *56–7*
essential oils 6, 96, 97, 122, *122*
Eugenia aromatica 121
Evernia purpuracea 121
exotic wood mix 46

F

Filipendula hexapetala 111
  F. palmata 103
  F. rubra 103
  F. ulmaria 103
fixatives 9, 96, 97, 120, *120–1*
fleabane 22
flowers:
  arrangements 57, *57,* 76, *76–81*
  drying 90, *90–5,* 93
  pomanders 75
  scented 86–9
Fortunella japonica 118
fragrant-root potpourri 36
frankincense 6, *120, 122*
fruit 46, *94,* 116, *116–19*
  citrus fruit potpourri 48
  drying 93
fuchsias 94, *94*
Fuchsia magellanica 94

G

galbanum 120
garden flowers 106, *106–9*
geranium (scented-leaf) 18, *18,*
    89, *104, 110*
  geranium oil *50*
  geranium roots 120
  rose and scented-leaf geranium
    potpourri 16
Geranium procurrens 86
Geum urbanum 113
gorse 22
  heather and gorse-flower
    mix 24
grapefruit peel *118*
Greek perfumiers 6
gum benzoin 96, 120, *120*
gum olibanum 46
Gunnera 87

H

handkerchief cases 11, *71*
hang-drying 90, *90–2*
harvesting flowers 89
hawthorn berries 116, *117*
heather and gorse-flower mix 24
Heliotropium peruvianum 89
Helleborus corsicus 88
Hemerocallis 106
herb bennet *113*
herbs *42,* 96
  country gardens *34*
  easy sweet-herb mix 20
  herb and lavender mix 37
  herb potpourri 7
  moist method potpourri *50*
  pillows 64–71, *64–71*
  rich mix 67
  spicy herb mix 20
  strongly scented 104, *104–5*
  subtly scented 102, *102–3*
  sweet-bag mix 59
  sweet-scented 18, *18–21*
honeysuckle oil *22*
hops *115*
horsemint *105*
Humulus lupulus 115
hydrangeas 42, 95, *95, 107*
Hypericum patulum 110

I

ilang ilang oil 46, *46,* 120
Illicium verum 112
Inula magnifica 103, 113
Iris florentina 120

J

jasmine oil *42*
Jerusalem sage *110*
jonquil 30
juniper 22, 110, *111, 115*
Juniperus communis 111, 115

K

Knautia macedonica 107
knotweed *109*
kumquat peel *118*

L

labdanum 120
lace cushions 68, *68–9*
lady's mantle 106, *108*
larkspur 106, *109*
Lavandula angustifolia 104
  L. stoechas 104
Lavatera arborea 95
lavender 56, 96, 104, *104*
  autumn potpourri 30, *30*
  country-garden mix 34, *34*
  exotic wood mix 46, *46*
  herb and lavender mix 37
  lavender bundles 76–7
  lavender mix 50, *50*
  lavender oil *14, 18, 22, 30, 46, 50, 122*
  lemon mix 18, *18*
  mixed-flower potpourri 22, *22*
  peacock potpourri 42, *42*
  rich rose potpourri 14, *14*
  rose and lavender bags 84
  rose and oakmoss potpourri 26, *26*
leaves 110, *110–11*
  drying 93
lemon balm *103*
  lemon mix 53
  marigold, lemon and mint mix 36
lemon oil 18
lemon peel 46, 118, *119*
lemon thyme *102*
lemon verbena *14,* 18, *18,* 120
  lemon mix 18, 53
lichen *89,* 120
lime peel 118, *119*
Linaria dalmatica 106
logwood chips *114*
loosestrife *107*
love-in-a-mist *108*
Lythrum virgatum 107

M

mace *22, 114*
maceration 122
Malus floribunda 94, 117
  M. purpurea 94
  M. robusta 117
marigolds 89, *108*
  marigold, lemon and mint mix 36
marjoram 18, *18,* 22, 26, 50
marjoram oil 120
marsh-mallow *105*
masterwort 108, *109*
materials 56–7, *56–7*
Matteuccia struthiopteris 111
meadow sage *102*
meadowsweet 18, *87*

Acknowledgments

The author would like to thank all the people at Dorling Kindersley who have so enthusiastically made this book possible. Jane Laing, my editor, for her understanding of the project, her support, and her professionalism; Gill Della Casa, my art editor, whose talent has been so skillfully manipulated in the design of the book, and to everyone else at Dorling Kindersley who has worked hard behind the scenes. I would like to extend a very special thank you to Geoff Dann for all the lovely photographs and for his understanding and appreciation of my craft and garden. Tony and Eira Hibbert allowed me to pick armfuls of luscious and varied hydrangeas from their beautiful garden, and I thank them for their contribution to the potpourris of this book. Peter Paris gave me dozens of beautiful roses for which I sincerely thank him. Sally Compton, of Cornish Herbs, picked me bunches of any lovely herb that took my fancy, and to Sally I am extremely grateful. Kathy Thomas helped me with my sewing at a moment's notice and to her I also express my gratitude. Finally, a very special thank you to my husband, Bob, who often cleared a path through the family, pets and even the garden, thus giving me a measure of peace and quiet in which to gather my flowers, make my potpourris and write my text.

Dorling Kindersley would like to thank Malcolm Hillier for supplying some beautiful flowers and for allowing us to photograph in his house; Mrs Edith Piper for her hospitality; Hilary Bird for the index; Richard Bird for verifying plant names; Linda Drake, Jean Flynn and Roger Smoothy for their help with proof-reading; Kate Grant and Monika Rollmann for keying-in; and Teresa Solomon for seeing the book through production.